EINKORN.

A Cookbook Celebrating the Beauty of Heritage Wheat

by

Wade T. Slavin

Baking Tips:

The cookbook provides expert tips and techniques to achieve the best results, whether you're making einkorn bread, muffins, or pancakes. It covers kneading, proofing, and baking times specific to einkorn flour.

Health Consciousness:

Many people are increasingly looking for healthier and more sustainable food options. The "Einkorn Cookbook" taps into this trend, promoting using an ancient grain that is easier to digest for some, potentially reducing gluten-related discomfort.

Culinary Inspiration:

Beyond the basics, this cookbook encourages culinary experimentation. It inspires readers to think creatively and adapt einkorn to their favorite recipes, allowing for a personalized approach to cooking with this unique grain.

Beautiful Photography:

The cookbook is often enhanced with stunning photography that captures the essence of einkorn-based dishes. The visuals not only inspire but also make the recipes more accessible.

Einkorn Berry Breakfast Bowl:

Ingredients:

- 1 cup einkorn berries
- 2 cups milk (or a dairy-free alternative)
- 1/4 cup honey or maple syrup
- 1 cup mixed berries (strawberries, blueberries, raspberries)
- 1/4 cup chopped nuts (almonds, walnuts, or pecans)
- 1/2 teaspoon vanilla extract

Instructions:

1. Drain the einkorn berries after giving them a cold water rinse.
2. Combine the milk and einkorn berries in a saucepan. Bring to a boil, lower the heat to a simmer, cover the pot, and cook for about 25 to 30 minutes until the einkorn berries are soft and the sauce has thickened.
3. Add the vanilla essence and honey (or maple syrup).
4. Spoon the einkorn berry mixture into bowls and garnish with chopped nuts and mixed berries.
5. Present warm and savor!

Einkorn Pancakes with Maple Syrup:

Ingredients:

- 1 cup einkorn flour
- Two tablespoons sugar
- One teaspoon of baking powder
- 1/2 teaspoon baking soda
- 1/4 teaspoon salt
- 1 cup buttermilk
- One egg
- Two tablespoons melted butter

- Maple syrup for serving

Instructions:

1. Combine the einkorn flour, sugar, baking soda, baking powder, and salt in a mixing dish.
2. Combine the buttermilk, egg, and melted butter in a separate basin.
3. Mix the dry ingredients briefly after adding the liquid components.
4. Lightly grease a griddle or skillet and heat it over medium-high heat.
5. For each pancake, spoon 1/4 cup of batter onto the griddle.
6. Once bubbles appear on the surface, flip the food over and cook until both sides are golden brown.
7. Add maple syrup to the food.
8.

Einkorn Blueberry Muffins:

Ingredients:

- 1 1/2 cups einkorn flour
- 1/2 cup sugar
- Two teaspoons of baking powder
- 1/2 teaspoon salt
- 1/2 cup milk
- 1/4 cup vegetable oil
- One egg
- 1 cup fresh or frozen blueberries

Instructions:

1. Line a muffin pan with paper liners and preheat the oven to 375°F (190°C).

2. Combine the einkorn flour, sugar, baking soda, and salt in a mixing dish.
3. Combine the milk, vegetable oil, and egg in a separate bowl.
4. Mix the dry ingredients briefly after adding the liquid components.
5. Slowly incorporate the blueberries.
6. Evenly distribute the batter among the muffin tins.
7. Bake the muffins for 20 to 25 minutes or until a toothpick inserted in the center comes out clean.
8. Let the muffins cool completely before serving.

Einkorn Banana Bread:

Ingredients:
- 2-3 ripe bananas, mashed
- 1/3 cup melted butter
- 1 cup sugar
- One egg, beaten
- One teaspoon of vanilla extract
- One teaspoon of baking soda
- Pinch of salt
- 1 1/2 cups einkorn flour

Instructions:
1. Grease a loaf pan and set your oven to 350°F (175°C).
2. Use a fork to mash the ripe bananas in a mixing basin.
3. Combine the melted butter with the banana puree.
4. Combine the sugar, vanilla essence, and the beaten egg.
5. Add the salt and baking soda to the batter and whisk.
6. Add the einkorn flour and blend only until combined.
7. Fill the prepared loaf pan with the batter.

8. Bake for 60 to 65 minutes, or until a toothpick inserted in the center of the cake comes out clean.
9. Let the banana bread cool completely before cutting it.

Einkorn Pumpkin Spice Waffles:

Ingredients:

- 1 1/2 cups einkorn flour
- Two tablespoons sugar
- One tablespoon of baking powder
- 1/2 teaspoon salt
- One teaspoon ground cinnamon
- 1/2 teaspoon ground nutmeg
- 1/4 teaspoon ground cloves
- 1 cup milk
- 1/2 cup canned pumpkin puree
- Two large eggs
- Two tablespoons melted butter
- One teaspoon of vanilla extract

Instructions:

1. Set your waffle maker to the recommended temperature by the manufacturer.
2. Combine the einkorn flour, sugar, baking powder, salt, and spices in a mixing dish.
3. Combine the milk, pumpkin puree, eggs, melted butter, and vanilla essence in a separate basin.
4. Mix the dry ingredients briefly after adding the liquid components.
5. Lightly spray butter or nonstick cooking spray on the waffle iron.
6. Spoon the batter onto the waffle iron and cook it, following the directions provided by the manufacturer.

7. Top the pumpkin spice waffles with your preferred icing, whipped cream, or maple syrup.

Einkorn Sourdough Bread:

Ingredients:
- 1 cup active sourdough starter
- 3 cups einkorn flour
- 1 1/2 cups warm water
- 1 1/2 teaspoons salt

Instructions:
1. Combine warm water and the active sourdough starter in a large mixing basin.
2. Stir in the salt and einkorn flour until a sticky dough forms in the bowl.
3. Cover the bowl with a clean towel and leave it at room temperature for roughly 12 to 18 hours to allow the mixture to ferment and rise.
4. Once the fermentation process is complete, preheat your oven to 450°F (232°C) and place a Dutch oven or other oven-safe pot inside.
5. Carefully remove the heated pot from the oven, then add the dough.
6. Cover the saucepan with a lid and put it back in the oven.
7. Bake the bread with the cover off for an additional 15-20 minutes, or until it is golden brown and makes a hollow sound when tapped on the bottom, after baking it for 30 minutes with the lid on.
8. Let the bread cool completely before cutting.

Einkorn Baguettes:

Ingredients:

- 2 cups einkorn flour
- One teaspoon salt
- One teaspoon of active dry yeast
- 3/4 cup warm water

Instructions:

1. Combine the salt and einkorn flour in a mixing dish.
2. Dissolve the yeast in the warm water in a separate basin. About 5 minutes should pass for it to get foamy.
3. Add the yeast mixture to the flour mixture and stir until a doughy consistency is achieved.
4. To smooth the dough, knead it for about 5 minutes on a floured surface.
5. Put the dough in an oiled bowl, cover it with a cloth, and allow it to double in size for about one to two hours.
6. Set a baking stone or an upside-down baking sheet on the center rack of your 450°F (232°C) oven.
7. Punch down the dough that has risen and divide it into two pieces.
8. Construct a long baguette form from each half.
9. Lay the baguettes on a floured board and give them 15 minutes to rest.
10. Use a sharp knife to score the baguette tops.
11. Place the baguettes on the baking stone or sheet that has been heated.
12. Bake for 20 to 25 minutes or until golden brown and the bottoms sound hollow when tapped.
13. Let the baguettes cool completely before cutting.

Einkorn Garlic Knots:

Ingredients:

- 1 pound pizza dough (einkorn or regular)
- 1/4 cup unsalted butter, melted
- Two cloves garlic, minced
- Two tablespoons fresh parsley, chopped
- Salt to taste
- Grated Parmesan cheese (optional)

Instructions:

1. Set your oven to 400 degrees Fahrenheit (200 degrees Celsius) and cover a baking sheet with parchment paper.
2. Separate the pizza dough into 12 sections of equal size.
3. Create an 8-inch rope out of each section.
4. Knot each rope and set it on the baking sheet that has been prepared.
5. Combine the melted butter, minced garlic, parsley, and a dash of salt in a small bowl.
6. Spread the knots with the garlic butter mixture.
7. Bake the knots for 12 to 15 minutes or until golden brown.
8. If you'd like, you can top the knots with freshly grated Parmesan cheese while they're still hot.
9. Present warm and savor!

Einkorn Focaccia with Rosemary:

Ingredients:

- 2 1/2 cups einkorn flour
- One teaspoon salt
- One teaspoon sugar
- One packet (2 1/4 teaspoons) of active dry yeast

- 1 cup warm water
- 1/4 cup olive oil
- 1-2 sprigs fresh rosemary
- Coarse sea salt for sprinkling

Instructions:

1. Combine the einkorn flour, salt, and sugar in a mixing basin.
2. Dissolve the yeast in the warm water in a separate basin. About 5 minutes should pass for it to get foamy.
3. Combine the flour mixture with the yeast mixture and two tablespoons of olive oil. Until a dough forms, stir.
4. To smooth the dough, knead it for about 5 minutes on a floured surface.
5. Put the dough in an oiled bowl, cover it with a cloth, and allow it to double in size for about one to two hours.
6. Prepare a baking sheet with greasing and preheat the oven to 425°F (220°C).
7. Create a flat rectangle by pressing the dough that has risen onto the prepared baking sheet.
8. Make ridges on the dough's surface using your fingers.
9. Pour the remaining olive oil over the dough and top with coarse sea salt and fresh rosemary.
10. Bake the focaccia for 20 to 25 minutes or until golden brown.
11. Let it cool just a little before cutting.

Einkorn Ciabatta Rolls:

Ingredients:

- 2 cups einkorn flour
- One teaspoon salt
- 1/4 teaspoon active dry yeast

- 1 1/4 cups warm water

Instructions:

1. In a mixing bowl, combine the salt and einkorn flour.
2. In another bowl, liquefy the yeast in the heated water. It should get frothy after around five minutes.
3. Stir the flour mixture and yeast mixture until it has a dough consistency.
4. Cover the bowl with plastic wrap and leave it at room temperature for 12 to 18 hours to allow the mixture to ferment and rise.
5. Position a baking sheet or stone on the middle rack of your 450°F (232°C) oven.
6. Scatter a thick layer of flour over the dough after scraping it onto a clean surface.
7. Divide the dough into four equal pieces, then roll out each piece to form an oval.
8. Set the rolls on a cookie sheet that has been coated with flour.
9. Score the tops of the rolls with a sharp knife.
10. Place the baking sheet on the stone or heated baking sheet in the oven.
11. Bake the rolls in the oven for twenty to twenty-five minutes or until crisp and golden brown.
12. Allow the ciabatta rolls to cool before serving.

Einkorn Garlic Bread:

Ingredients:

- One loaf of einkorn bread (store-bought or homemade)
- 1/2 cup unsalted butter, softened
- 3-4 cloves garlic, minced
- Two tablespoons fresh parsley, chopped (optional)
- Salt to taste

Instructions:
1. Set the oven's temperature to 375°F (190°C).
2. Horizontally cut the einkorn bread in half.
3. Combine the softened butter, minced garlic, parsley (if using), and a dash of salt in a mixing dish.
4. Cover the sliced sides of the bread evenly with the garlic butter mixture.
5. Reassemble the two pieces to make the bread.
6. Fold aluminum foil around the bread.
7. Bake the bread in the oven for 10 to 15 minutes or until it is thoroughly heated through and the butter has melted.
8. You can leave the foil open for the last few minutes to slightly crisp up the bread.
9. Slice the garlic bread and serve it hot.

Einkorn Pretzels:

Ingredients:
- 1 1/2 cups warm water
- One packet (2 1/4 teaspoons) of active dry yeast
- 4 cups einkorn flour
- One teaspoon salt
- Two tablespoons sugar
- 2/3 cup baking soda
- Coarse sea salt for sprinkling

Instructions:
1. Combine the yeast and warm water in a basin. About 5 minutes should pass for it to get foamy.
2. Combine the einkorn flour, salt, and sugar in another basin.

3. Combine the flour and yeast mixture and knead the dough until smooth.
4. Let the dough rest for about 30 minutes while covered.
5. Set a baking sheet on your oven's 450°F (232°C) lowest setting and preheat it.
6. Make 12 equal bits of the dough and roll each into a rope.
7. Cut each rope into a pretzel shape, then arrange it on the baking sheet that has been prepared.
8. Bring 10 cups of water and the baking soda to a boil in a big pot.
9. After each pretzel has boiled for 30 seconds, put it back on the baking pan.
10. Finish with a sprinkle of sea salt.
11. Bake the pretzels for 12 to 15 minutes or until golden brown.
12. Let them cool just a little before serving.

Einkorn Grilled Cheese Sandwich:

Ingredients:
- Four slices of einkorn bread
- Two tablespoons unsalted butter softened
- 1 1/2 cups shredded cheddar cheese or your favorite cheese

Instructions:
1. Heat a skillet or griddle to a low temperature.
2. Butter one side of every einkorn bread slice.
3. Lay down two pieces of bread with the buttery side up on a smooth surface.
4. Evenly distribute the cheese between the slices of bread.

5. Place the remaining slices of bread, butter side up, on top.
6. Arrange the sandwiches on the hot griddle or skillet.
7. Cook for 3 to 4 minutes on each side or until the cheese has melted and the bread is golden brown.
8. Turn off the heat, slice, and serve immediately.

Einkorn Tomato Basil Bruschetta:

Ingredients:

- 4 slices of einkorn baguette or ciabatta
- Two ripe tomatoes, diced
- 1/4 cup fresh basil leaves, chopped
- Two cloves garlic, minced
- Two tablespoons extra-virgin olive oil
- Salt and pepper to taste
- Balsamic glaze for drizzling (optional)

Instructions:

1. Set the oven's temperature to 400°F (200°C).
2. Arrange the slices of einkorn bread on a baking sheet and toast them in the oven for 5 to 7 minutes or until crisp and gently browned.
3. Combine the diced tomatoes, chopped basil, minced garlic, and olive oil in a mixing dish. To taste, add salt and pepper to the food.
4. Spread the toasted slices of einkorn bread with the tomato mixture.
5. You could put some balsamic glaze on top.
6. Immediately serve the tomato basil bruschetta.

Einkorn Caesar Salad:

Ingredients:

- One head of romaine lettuce, chopped
- 1/2 cup croutons (einkorn or store-bought)
- 1/2 cup grated Parmesan cheese
- Caesar dressing (store-bought or homemade)

Instructions:

1. Combine the romaine lettuce, croutons, and grated Parmesan cheese in a big salad dish.
2. Dress the salad with the Caesar dressing.
3. Stir the salad so that all of the ingredients are coated.
4. Present the Caesar salad right away.
5.

Einkorn Spinach and Strawberry Salad:

Ingredients:

- 6 cups baby spinach leaves
- 1 1/2 cups fresh strawberries, sliced
- 1/2 cup crumbled feta cheese
- 1/4 cup chopped pecans or walnuts
- Balsamic vinaigrette dressing

Instructions:

1. Place the baby spinach, strawberry slices, feta cheese crumbles, and chopped almonds in a large salad bowl.
2. Dress with a balsamic vinaigrette.
3. Stir the salad so that all of the ingredients are coated.
4. Present the strawberry and spinach salad right away.

Einkorn Greek Salad:

Ingredients:

- 4 cups chopped romaine lettuce
- One cucumber, diced
- 1 cup cherry tomatoes, halved
- 1/2 red onion, thinly sliced
- 1/2 cup Kalamata olives, pitted and sliced
- 1/2 cup crumbled feta cheese
- Greek dressing (store-bought or homemade)

Instructions:

1. Place the chopped romaine lettuce, diced cucumber, cherry tomatoes, red onion, Kalamata olives, and crumbled feta cheese in a large salad dish.
2. Add a Greek dressing drizzle.
3. Stir the salad so that all of the ingredients are coated.
4. Present the Greek salad right away.

Einkorn Caprese Salad:

Ingredients:

- Four ripe tomatoes, sliced
- 8 ounces fresh mozzarella cheese, sliced
- Fresh basil leaves
- Extra-virgin olive oil
- Balsamic glaze
- Salt and pepper to taste

Instructions:

1. Alternately, arrange the tomato and mozzarella slices on a serving dish.
2. Sandwich thin slices of tomato and mozzarella with fresh basil.

3. Drizzle the salad with extra virgin olive oil and balsamic glaze.
4. To taste, add salt and pepper to the dish.
5. Present the Caprese salad right away.

Einkorn Quinoa Salad:

Ingredients:

- 1 cup einkorn
- 2 cups water
- 1 1/2 cups cooked quinoa
- 1/2 cup diced cucumber
- 1/2 cup diced red bell pepper
- 1/2 cup diced red onion
- 1/4 cup chopped fresh parsley
- 1/4 cup crumbled feta cheese
- Juice of 1 lemon
- Two tablespoons extra-virgin olive oil
- Salt and pepper to taste

Instructions:

1. Drain the einkorn after giving it a cold water rinse.
2. Combine the einkorn and water in a saucepan. Bring to a boil, lower the heat to a simmer, cover the pot, and cook for about 25 to 30 minutes until the einkorn is cooked and the water has been absorbed.
3. Combine the cooked einkorn and quinoa with the diced cucumber, red bell pepper, red onion, fresh parsley, and crumbled feta cheese in a big bowl.
4. Combine the lemon juice and extra virgin olive oil in a small bowl.
5. After adding the dressing to the salad, mix it to properly distribute the ingredients.

6. To taste, add salt and pepper.
7. Present the einkorn quinoa salad cold or at room temperature.

Einkorn Tabbouleh:

Ingredients:
- 1/2 cup einkorn
- 1 cup water
- 1 cup chopped fresh parsley
- 1/4 cup chopped fresh mint leaves
- Two tomatoes, diced
- 1/2 cucumber, diced
- 1/4 cup diced red onion
- Juice of 1 lemon
- Two tablespoons extra-virgin olive oil
- Salt and pepper to taste

Instructions:
1. Drain the einkorn after giving it a cold water rinse.
2. Combine the einkorn and water in a saucepan. Bring to a boil, lower the heat to a simmer, cover the pot, and cook for about 25 to 30 minutes until the einkorn is cooked and the water has been absorbed.
3. Combine the cooked einkorn with the diced tomatoes, cucumber, red onion, fresh mint leaves, and chopped fresh parsley in a big bowl.
4. Combine the lemon juice and extra virgin olive oil in a small bowl.
5. After adding the dressing, mix the tabbouleh salad to properly distribute the ingredients.
6. To taste, add salt and pepper.

7. Present the einkorn tabbouleh salad cold or at room temperature.

Einkorn Potato Salad:

Ingredients:

- 3 cups diced cooked potatoes
- 1/2 cup diced celery
- 1/4 cup diced red onion
- 1/4 cup chopped fresh parsley
- 1/2 cup mayonnaise
- Two tablespoons of Dijon mustard
- One tablespoon of apple cider vinegar
- Salt and pepper to taste
- Paprika for garnish (optional)

Instructions:

1. Combine the diced cooked potatoes, celery, red onion, and freshly cut parsley in a big bowl.
2. Combine the mayonnaise, Dijon mustard, and apple cider vinegar in a small bowl.
3. Add the dressing to the potato salad, tossing to uniformly coat the ingredients.
4. To taste, add salt and pepper to the dish.
5. If preferred, add paprika as a garnish.
6. Present the chilled Einkorn potato salad.

Einkorn Coleslaw:

Ingredients:

For the Coleslaw:

- 4 cups shredded green cabbage
- 1 cup shredded purple cabbage
- 1 cup grated carrots
- 1/2 cup thinly sliced green onions
- 1/4 cup chopped fresh parsley

For the Dressing:

- 1/2 cup mayonnaise
- Two tablespoons of apple cider vinegar
- Two tablespoons honey
- One teaspoon of Dijon mustard
- Salt and black pepper to taste

Instructions:

1. Combine the grated carrots, shredded green and purple cabbage, sliced green onions, and fresh parsley in a sizable mixing dish. To get a smooth mixture, toss the ingredients together.
2. Combine the mayonnaise, apple cider vinegar, honey, Dijon mustard, salt, and black pepper in a separate bowl. Blend the dressing until it's smooth and evenly distributed.
3. In the big bowl with the coleslaw mixture, pour the dressing.
4. Gently combine the coleslaw and dressing with a spatula or large spoon, and coat all the veggies in the dressing.

5. At least 30 minutes before serving, cover the coleslaw and place it in the refrigerator. The flavors might converge when chilled.
6. Whether you're having a picnic, a cookout, or a family supper, serve the Einkorn Coleslaw as a side dish.

Einkorn Waldorf Salad:

Ingredients:

For the Salad:

- 2 cups diced cooked chicken breast
- 2 cups diced apples (such as Granny Smith)
- 1 cup chopped celery
- 1/2 cup chopped walnuts
- 1/2 cup seedless grapes, halved

For the Dressing:

- 1/2 cup mayonnaise
- Two tablespoons of Greek yogurt
- One tablespoon honey
- One tablespoon of lemon juice
- Salt and black pepper to taste

Instructions:

1. Combine the diced chicken, apples, celery, chopped walnuts, and half of the grapes in a large mixing dish.
2. To make the dressing, combine the mayonnaise, Greek yogurt, honey, lemon juice, salt, and black pepper in a separate small bowl.

3. Drizzle the salad mixture in the big bowl with the dressing.
4. Gently toss the ingredients in the salad with the dressing until they are all coated.
5. At least 30 minutes before serving, place the Einkorn Waldorf Salad in the refrigerator.
6. Offer chilled as an excellent salad.

Einkorn Roasted Vegetable Salad:

Ingredients:

For the Salad:

- 4 cups mixed roasted vegetables (such as bell peppers, zucchini, cherry tomatoes, and red onion)
- 1 cup cooked and cooled Einkorn wheat berries
- 1/2 cup crumbled feta cheese
- Two tablespoons fresh basil leaves, chopped

For the Dressing:

- Three tablespoons extra-virgin olive oil
- Two tablespoons of balsamic vinegar
- One clove of garlic, minced
- Salt and black pepper to taste

Instructions:

1. Set the oven's temperature to 400°F (200°C). Add salt, pepper, and a splash of olive oil to the mixture of vegetables. 20 to 25 minutes of roasting should be plenty to get them soft and slightly browned. Ensure that they reach room temperature.

2. Combine the roasted veggies, cooked Einkorn wheat berries, feta cheese crumbles, and basil leaves in a bowl.
3. To create the dressing, combine the extra virgin olive oil, balsamic vinegar, minced garlic, salt, and pepper in a small bowl.
4. Pour the salad dressing over everything and toss to mix.
5. Offer the Einkorn Roasted Vegetable Salad as a filling side dish or a healthy main dish.

Einkorn Asian Noodle Salad:

Ingredients:

For the Salad:

- 8 oz (about 2 cups) cooked Einkorn noodles, cooled
- 1 cup shredded Napa cabbage
- 1 cup thinly sliced red bell pepper
- 1 cup shredded carrots
- 1/2 cup chopped cucumber
- 1/4 cup chopped fresh cilantro
- 1/4 cup chopped green onions
- 1/4 cup chopped peanuts (optional)

For the Dressing:

- 1/4 cup soy sauce
- Two tablespoons of rice vinegar
- One tablespoon of sesame oil
- One tablespoon honey
- One clove of garlic, minced
- One teaspoon of grated fresh ginger

- Red pepper flakes (optional, for heat)

Instructions:

1. Place the cooked and cooled Einkorn noodles, Napa cabbage shreds, red bell pepper slices, carrot shreds, cucumber chunks, cilantro, and green onions in a large bowl.
2. Combine the soy sauce, rice vinegar, sesame oil, honey, grated ginger, and red pepper flakes (if using) in a different bowl.
3. Add the salad ingredients to the big bowl along with the dressing and stir to mix.
4. For more crunch, if desired, sprinkle chopped peanuts on top.
5. At least 30 minutes before serving, place the Einkorn Asian Noodle Salad in the refrigerator.
6. Serve chilled as a delectable salad with an Asian flair.

Einkorn Chicken Caesar Salad:

Ingredients:

For the Salad:

- 2 cups cooked and diced chicken breast
- 6 cups chopped romaine lettuce
- 1/2 cup croutons
- 1/4 cup grated Parmesan cheese

For the Caesar Dressing:

- 1/2 cup mayonnaise

- 1/4 cup grated Parmesan cheese
- Two tablespoons of lemon juice
- One clove of garlic, minced
- One teaspoon of Dijon mustard
- Salt and black pepper to taste

Instructions:

1. Combine the diced chicken, romaine lettuce, croutons, and grated Parmesan cheese in a big salad dish.
2. To create the Caesar dressing, combine the mayonnaise, grated Parmesan cheese, lemon juice, chopped garlic, Dijon mustard, salt, and black pepper in another bowl.
3. Drizzle the salad with the dressing and toss to evenly coat the contents.
4. Serve the traditional and filling Einkorn Chicken Caesar Salad.

Einkorn BLT Sandwich:

Ingredients:

- Eight slices of Einkorn bread
- Eight slices of bacon, cooked until crispy
- Four lettuce leaves
- Two ripe tomatoes, thinly sliced
- 1/4 cup mayonnaise
- Salt and black pepper to taste

Instructions:

1. Slices of Einkorn bread should be lightly browned during toasting.
2. On one side of each slice of bread, equally spread mayonnaise.

3. Arrange four slices of bread with the bacon, lettuce leaves, and tomato slices on top.
4. Season the tomatoes with a bit of salt and black pepper.
5. Place the remaining bread slices, mayonnaise side down, on top of each sandwich.
6. Cut your delectable Einkorn BLT Sandwiches in half diagonally and serve them.

Einkorn Turkey Club Sandwich:

Ingredients:
- 12 slices of Einkorn bread
- Eight slices of turkey
- Eight slices of bacon, cooked until crispy
- Four lettuce leaves
- Four slices of tomato
- Four tablespoons mayonnaise
- Salt and black pepper to taste

Instructions:
1. Slices of Einkorn bread should be lightly browned during toasting.
2. On one side of each slice of bread, equally spread mayonnaise.
3. Arrange the turkey, bacon, lettuce, and tomato in three layers.
4. Add a dash of black pepper and salt to the tomato slices.
5. Place the remaining bread slices, mayonnaise side down, on top of each sandwich.
6. Cut each sandwich into quarters and secure it with toothpicks.

7. Present your Einkorn Turkey Club Sandwiches to guests as a traditional and filling lunch.

Einkorn Veggie Wrap:

Ingredients:

For the Wrap:

- 4 large Einkorn tortillas
- 2 cups mixed salad greens
- 1 cup shredded carrots
- 1 cup sliced cucumber
- 1/2 cup thinly sliced red bell pepper
- 1/2 cup sliced avocado
- 1/4 cup crumbled feta cheese (optional)

For the Hummus Spread:

- 1 cup hummus (store-bought or homemade)
- Juice of 1 lemon
- Salt and black pepper to taste

Instructions:

1. To make the hummus spread, combine the hummus, lemon juice, salt, and black pepper in a small bowl.
2. Arrange the Einkorn tortillas and evenly distribute the hummus mixture over each one.
3. Arrange the salad greens, carrots, cucumber, red bell pepper, and avocado slices in a uniform layer on top of the hummus mixture.
4. If preferred, top the vegetables with crumbled feta cheese.

5. Roll up each tortilla and tuck the sides in to make a wrap.
6. Cut your Einkorn Veggie Wraps in half diagonally and serve them...

Einkorn Chicken Salad Sandwich:

Ingredients:

For the Chicken Salad:

- 2 cups cooked and shredded chicken breast
- 1/2 cup mayonnaise
- 1/4 cup chopped celery
- Two tablespoons chopped red onion
- One tablespoon of chopped fresh parsley
- Salt and black pepper to taste

For the Sandwich:

- Eight slices of Einkorn bread
- Lettuce leaves
- Tomato slices

Instructions:

1. Combine the shredded chicken, mayonnaise, celery, red onion, parsley, salt, and black pepper in a mixing dish. Mix everything thoroughly until mixed.
2. Top 4 slices of Einkorn bread with the chicken salad mixture.
3. Add tomato slices and lettuce leaves on top.
4. To assemble sandwiches, add the remaining four slices of bread on top.

5. To serve your Einkorn Chicken Salad Sandwiches, cut them in half diagonally.

Einkorn Egg Salad Sandwich:

Ingredients:

For the Egg Salad:

- Six hard-boiled eggs, peeled and chopped
- 1/4 cup mayonnaise
- Two tablespoons of Dijon mustard
- Two tablespoons chopped fresh chives
- Salt and black pepper to taste

For the Sandwich:

- Eight slices of Einkorn bread
- Lettuce leaves
- Sliced tomatoes

Instructions:

1. Combine the chopped hard-boiled eggs with the mayonnaise, Dijon mustard, chopped chives, salt, and pepper in a mixing dish. Mix all of the ingredients thoroughly.
2. Cover four pieces of Einkorn bread with the egg salad mixture.
3. Add sliced tomatoes and lettuce leaves on top.
4. To assemble sandwiches, add the remaining four slices of bread on top.
5. To serve your Einkorn Egg Salad Sandwiches, cut them in half diagonally.

Einkorn Avocado Toast:

Ingredients:

- Two slices of Einkorn bread toasted
- One ripe avocado
- Salt and black pepper to taste
- Red pepper flakes (optional)
- Olive oil (for drizzling)
- Lemon juice (for drizzling)

Instructions:

1. Scoop the flesh from the half-ripe avocado, remove the pit, and place it in a basin.
2. Use a fork to mash the avocado until it has the desired creaminess.
3. Add salt, black pepper, and a dash of red pepper flakes to the mashed avocado (if you prefer it spicy).
4. Evenly spread the avocado mixture across the toasted slices of Einkorn bread.
5. Squeeze some lemon juice and olive oil over the avocado.
6. Offer your Einkorn Avocado Toast as a speedy and wholesome breakfast option.

Einkorn Tomato Soup:

Ingredients:

- Two tablespoons of olive oil
- One onion, chopped
- Two cloves garlic, minced
- Two cans (28 ounces each) of whole peeled tomatoes
- 1 cup vegetable broth
- One teaspoon of dried basil

- Salt and black pepper to taste
- 1/2 cup heavy cream (optional)

Instructions:

1. Place a big pot over medium heat and warm the olive oil. Sauté the minced garlic and onion until they are transparent after adding them.
2. Fill the saucepan with the dried basil, vegetable broth, canned tomatoes (and their liquids), salt, and black pepper. After bringing to a boil, turn down the heat, cover, and simmer for 15 to 20 minutes.
3. Puree the mixture with an immersion blender or in a blender until smooth.
4. Add the heavy cream (if using) and bring the soup back to a simmer. Warm up completely without boiling.
5. If preferred, top your heated Einkorn Tomato Soup with fresh basil.

Einkorn Minestrone Soup:

Ingredients:

- Two tablespoons of olive oil
- One onion, chopped
- Two cloves garlic, minced
- Two carrots diced
- Two celery stalks, diced
- One zucchini, diced
- 1 cup cooked Einkorn wheat berries
- One can (14 ounces) diced tomatoes
- 6 cups vegetable broth
- One teaspoon of dried basil
- One teaspoon dried oregano
- Salt and black pepper to taste

- 1 cup chopped spinach or kale
- 1/4 cup grated Parmesan cheese (optional)

Instructions:

1. Place a big pot over medium heat and warm the olive oil. Add the diced carrots, celery, zucchini, onion, and minced garlic. Sauté the vegetables until they start to soften.
2. Add salt, pepper, dried basil, dried oregano, chopped tomatoes with juice, cooked Einkorn wheat berries, and vegetable broth.
3. Bring the soup to a boil before boiling it to a simmer for 15 to 20 minutes or until the veggies are fork-tender.
4. Add the spinach or kale that has been chopped, and simmer for an additional 5 minutes or until wilted.
5. Top your hot Einkorn Minestrone Soup with grated Parmesan cheese if desired.

Einkorn Butternut Squash Soup:

Ingredients:

- One medium butternut squash, peeled, seeded, and diced
- One onion, chopped
- Two cloves garlic, minced
- Two carrots diced
- Two celery stalks, diced
- 4 cups vegetable broth
- One teaspoon of dried thyme
- Salt and black pepper to taste
- 1/2 cup heavy cream (optional)
- Fresh parsley or chives for garnish (optional)

Instructions:

1. Heat some olive oil in a big pot over medium heat. Add the diced carrots, celery, minced garlic, and chopped onion. Sauté the vegetables until they are tender and aromatic.
2. Fill the pot with the diced butternut squash, vegetable broth, dried thyme, salt, and pepper. Bring to a boil, lower the heat to a simmer, and cook the butternut squash for 20 to 25 minutes, depending on how tender you like.
3. Puree the soup with an immersion blender or until it is smooth.
4. Add the heavy cream (if using) and bring the soup back to a simmer. Warm up entirely without boiling.
5. Garnish your Einkorn Butternut Squash Soup with fresh chives or parsley.

Einkorn Potato Leek Soup:

Ingredients:

- Two tablespoons butter
- Two leeks, white and light green parts, chopped
- Four potatoes, peeled and diced
- 4 cups vegetable broth
- One bay leaf
- Salt and black pepper to taste
- 1/2 cup heavy cream (optional)
- Chopped chives for garnish (optional)

Instructions:

1. Melt the butter in a big pot over medium heat. Leeks that have been chopped should be added and sautéed until soft and transparent.

2. Fill the saucepan with the diced potatoes, vegetable broth, bay leaf, salt, and pepper. The potatoes should be cooked after 20 to 25 minutes of simmering over low heat after bringing to a boil.
3. Remove the bay leaf and purée the soup in a blender or immersion blender until smooth.
4. Add the heavy cream (if using) and bring the soup back to a simmer. Warm up entirely without boiling.
5. Top your Einkorn Potato Leek Soup with chopped chives before serving.

Einkorn Gazpacho:

Ingredients:
- Six ripe tomatoes, chopped
- One cucumber, peeled and chopped
- One red bell pepper, chopped
- One red onion, chopped
- 3 cups tomato juice
- 1/4 cup red wine vinegar
- 1/4 cup olive oil
- Two cloves garlic, minced
- Salt and black pepper to taste
- Fresh basil or cilantro for garnish (optional)

Instructions:
1. Combine the finely diced tomatoes, cucumber, red bell pepper, and red onion in a large bowl.
2. Blend or process the tomato juice, red wine vinegar, olive oil, minced garlic, salt, and black pepper with the remaining half of the vegetable combination until smooth.

3. Add the remaining chopped veggies to the dish containing the pureed mixture. Mix thoroughly.
4. Before serving, the Einkorn Gazpacho should be chilled in the fridge for at least two hours.
5. If desired, top the gazpacho with fresh cilantro or basil before serving.

Einkorn Lentil Soup:

Ingredients:

- 1 cup dried green or brown lentils, rinsed and drained
- One onion, chopped
- Two carrots diced
- Two celery stalks, diced
- Two cloves garlic, minced
- 6 cups vegetable broth
- One teaspoon of ground cumin
- 1/2 teaspoon ground coriander
- Salt and black pepper to taste
- Juice of 1 lemon
- Fresh parsley for garnish (optional)

Instructions:

1. Sauté the diced carrots, celery, onion, and minced garlic in a bit of olive oil in a big pot until the veggies are tender and fragrant.
2. Fill the saucepan with the washed lentils, vegetable broth, cumin, coriander, salt, and black pepper. Bring to a boil, lower the heat, and simmer the lentils for 30 to 35 minutes or until cooked through.
3. Add the lemon juice and, if necessary, add more salt and black pepper to taste.

4. If preferred, top your heated Einkorn Lentil Soup with fresh parsley.

Einkorn Chicken Noodle Soup:

Ingredients:
- Two tablespoons of olive oil
- One onion, chopped
- Two carrots diced
- Two celery stalks, diced
- Two cloves garlic, minced
- 6 cups chicken broth
- 2 cups cooked and shredded chicken breast
- 2 cups cooked Einkorn noodles
- Salt and black pepper to taste
- Fresh parsley for garnish (optional)

Instructions:
1. Place a big pot over medium heat and warm the olive oil. Add the minced garlic, diced celery, carrots, and sliced onion. Sauté the vegetables until they are tender and aromatic.
2. Fill the kettle with the chicken broth and bring to a boil. For roughly 15 minutes, lower the heat and simmer the dish.
3. Add cooked Einkorn noodles and chicken that has been shredded. Continue to simmer for a further five minutes to fully heat the mixture.
4. To taste, add salt and black pepper to the soup.
5. If preferred, top your hot Einkorn Chicken Noodle Soup with fresh parsley.

Einkorn Chili:

Ingredients:

- 1 pound ground beef
- One medium onion, chopped
- One bell pepper, chopped
- Two cloves garlic, minced
- One can (14.5 ounces) diced tomatoes
- One can (15 ounces) tomato sauce
- One can (15 ounces) kidney beans, drained and rinsed
- One can (15 ounces) black beans, drained and rinsed
- One can (4 ounces) diced green chilies
- Two tablespoons of chili powder
- One teaspoon cumin
- One teaspoon paprika
- Salt and pepper to taste
- Optional toppings: shredded cheese, sour cream, chopped green onions, diced jalapeños

Instructions:

1. Brown the ground beef in a big saucepan or Dutch oven over medium-high heat, breaking it up as it cooks with a spoon. Whenever required, remove any extra fat.
2. Include the sliced bell pepper and onion with the browned beef in the pot. Cook the vegetables for 3 to 4 minutes or until they soften.
3. Add the minced garlic and stir, cooking for a further minute or until fragrant.
4. Fill the saucepan with the diced tomatoes, tomato sauce, black beans, kidney beans, diced green chilies, cumin, paprika, salt, and pepper. The items should be stirred together.

5. Increase the heat to a simmer before lowering it. For the flavors to combine, simmer it covered for at least 30 minutes. For an even fuller taste, boil it for longer.
6. After tasting the chili, add salt, pepper, or spices to adjust the flavors as desired.
7. Ladle the chili into bowls and serve it hot. Add your preferred toppings, such as sour cream, chopped green onions, shredded cheese, or sliced jalapenos.

Einkorn Vegetable Curry:

Ingredients:

- Two tablespoons of vegetable oil
- One onion, chopped
- Two cloves garlic, minced
- One tablespoon of ginger, minced
- Two tablespoons of curry powder
- One can (14 ounces) coconut milk
- 2 cups mixed vegetables (e.g., carrots, bell peppers, broccoli, and peas)
- 1 cup chickpeas, drained and rinsed
- Salt and pepper to taste
- Fresh cilantro leaves for garnish (optional)
- Cooked Einkorn rice for serving

Instructions:

1. Place a large skillet over medium heat and add the vegetable oil. Add the chopped onion and sauté for two to three minutes until it begins to soften.
2. Add the minced ginger and garlic and stir-fry for a further minute or so until fragrant.
3. Stir continuously for 1–2 minutes while adding the curry powder.

4. Pour the coconut milk in and boil the mixture.
5. Fill the skillet with the chickpeas and mixed veggies. Simmer the vegetables for 10 to 15 minutes or until they are soft.
6. To taste, add salt and pepper to the curry.
7. Spoon the cooked Einkorn rice over the vegetable curry, and if preferred, top with fresh cilantro leaves.

Einkorn Thai Green Curry:

Ingredients:

- 1 pound chicken breast or tofu, cubed (optional)
- 2 tablespoons green curry paste
- One can (14 ounces) coconut milk
- One red bell pepper, sliced
- One zucchini, sliced
- 1 cup green beans, trimmed
- One tablespoon of fish sauce (or soy sauce for a vegetarian option)
- One tablespoon of brown sugar
- Fresh basil leaves for garnish (optional)
- Cooked Einkorn rice for serving

Instructions:

1. Heat a little oil over medium-high heat in a large skillet or wok. Cook chicken or tofu, if using, until browned and thoroughly cooked. Take out of the pan and place aside.
2. Place the green curry paste in the same pan and heat for one minute until fragrant.
3. Add the coconut milk and boil for three minutes.

4. Include the green beans, zucchini, and red bell pepper in the pan. The vegetables should be cooked for 5-7 minutes or until they are soft.
5. Add the brown sugar and fish sauce. As needed, adjust the seasoning.
6. Return the chicken or tofu to the pan and boil for two to three minutes.
7. Top cooked Einkorn rice with the Thai green curry and, if preferred, fresh basil leaves.

Einkorn Red Lentil Curry:

Ingredients:

- 1 cup red lentils, rinsed and drained
- One onion, chopped
- Two cloves garlic, minced
- One tablespoon of curry powder
- One can (14 ounces) diced tomatoes
- One can (14 ounces) coconut milk
- 2 cups vegetable broth
- Salt and pepper to taste
- Fresh cilantro leaves for garnish (optional)
- Cooked Einkorn rice or naan bread for serving

Instructions:

1. Heat some oil in a big pot over medium heat. Add the chopped onion and sauté for two to three minutes until it begins to soften.
2. Add the curry powder and minced garlic. Cook until aromatic for one more minute.
3. Fill the pot with coconut milk, vegetable broth, diced tomatoes, and red lentils. To blend, stir.

4. Simmer the mixture for four minutes, then turn down the heat and cover. Allow the curry to boil for 20 to 25 minutes or until the lentils are tender.
5. To taste, add salt and pepper to the food.
6. Either serve the Red Lentil Curry with naan bread or overcooked Einkorn rice. If desired, garnish with fresh cilantro leaves.

Einkorn Chickpea Tikka Masala:

Ingredients:

- Two tablespoons of vegetable oil
- One onion, chopped
- Two cloves garlic, minced
- One tablespoon of ginger, minced
- One can (14 ounces) diced tomatoes
- One can (14 ounces) chickpeas, drained and rinsed
- 2 tablespoons tikka masala paste
- 1 cup coconut milk
- Salt and pepper to taste
- Fresh cilantro leaves for garnish (optional)
- Cooked Einkorn rice or naan bread for serving

Instructions:

1. Place a large skillet over medium heat and add the vegetable oil. Add the chopped onion and sauté for two to three minutes until it begins to soften.
2. Add the minced ginger and garlic and stir-fry for a further minute or so until fragrant.
3. Add the tikka masala paste and stir continuously for 1-2 minutes.
4. Add the chickpeas and diced tomatoes. For about five minutes, simmer.

5. Add the coconut milk and cook for 10 minutes to thicken the sauce.
6. To taste, add salt and pepper.
7. Top cooked Einkorn rice with the Chickpea Tikka Masala and naan bread. If desired, garnish with fresh cilantro leaves.

Einkorn Beef and Broccoli Stir-Fry:

Ingredients:

- 1 pound beef sirloin, thinly sliced
- 1/4 cup soy sauce
- Two tablespoons of oyster sauce
- Two cloves garlic, minced
- One teaspoon of ginger, minced
- One tablespoon of vegetable oil
- 2 cups broccoli florets
- Cooked Einkorn rice for serving

Instructions:

1. Combine the soy sauce, oyster sauce, ginger, and garlic in a bowl. Add the meat slices and let the mixture sit for at least 15 minutes.
2. Heat the vegetable oil over high heat in a wok or sizable skillet. Stir-fry the meat with the marinade for 2–3 minutes or until browned. From the pan, take out the beef, and set it aside.
3. Place the broccoli florets in the same pan and stir-fry for 2 to 3 minutes or until they are tender-crisp.
4. Add the cooked beef back to the pan and stir everything together.
5. Spoon the cooked Einkorn rice over the beef and broccoli stir-fry.

Einkorn Teriyaki Chicken:

Ingredients:

- 1 pound chicken breast or thighs, diced
- 1/2 cup teriyaki sauce
- Two tablespoons of soy sauce
- Two cloves garlic, minced
- One tablespoon of ginger, minced
- One tablespoon of vegetable oil
- 1 cup broccoli florets
- 1 cup sliced carrots
- Cooked Einkorn rice for serving
- Sesame seeds and chopped green onions for garnish (optional)

Instructions:

1. Combine the teriyaki sauce, soy sauce, ginger, and garlic in a bowl. Add the chicken cubes and let the mixture sit for at least 15 minutes.
2. In a sizable skillet over medium-high heat, warm the vegetable oil. Add the marinated chicken and cook for 5-7 minutes, or until done and just beginning to caramelize.
3. Take the chicken out of the skillet and place it aside.
4. Include the broccoli and carrots in the same pan. 3–4 minutes of stirring should be sufficient to achieve tender-crispness.
5. Add the marinade to the pan with the cooked chicken once more. Cook the chicken and vegetables for 2 to 3 minutes while stirring to coat.

6. Spoon cooked Einkorn rice over the Teriyaki Chicken. If desired, garnish with chopped green onions and sesame seeds.

Einkorn Vegetable Stir-Fry:

Ingredients:

- Two tablespoons of vegetable oil
- One onion, sliced
- Two cloves garlic, minced
- One red bell pepper, sliced
- One yellow bell pepper, sliced
- One green bell pepper, sliced
- 1 cup broccoli florets
- 1 cup snap peas
- 1/4 cup soy sauce
- Two tablespoons of oyster sauce
- Cooked Einkorn rice for serving

Instructions:

1. Heat the vegetable oil over high heat in a wok or sizable skillet—Stir-fry the chopped onion and garlic for one to two minutes or until fragrant.
2. Include the broccoli, snap peas, and bell pepper slices in the pan. Vegetables should be stir-fried for 3–4 minutes or until crisp-tender.
3. Combine the soy sauce and oyster sauce in a small basin. The sauce should be applied to the vegetables in a thin layer.
4. Stir-fry for a further 1-2 minutes to allow the sauce to gradually thicken.
5. Spoon the cooked Einkorn rice over the vegetable stir-fry.

Einkorn Fried Rice:

Ingredients:

- 2 cups cooked Einkorn rice, cold
- Two tablespoons of vegetable oil
- Two cloves garlic, minced
- 1/2 cup diced carrots
- 1/2 cup frozen peas
- Two eggs, beaten
- Two tablespoons of soy sauce
- 1/2 teaspoon sesame oil (optional)
- Sliced green onions for garnish (optional)

Instructions:

1. Heat the vegetable oil over medium-high heat in a sizable skillet or wok. Add the minced garlic and cook until fragrant, about 30 seconds.
2. Include the frozen peas and diced carrots in the pan. Vegetables should be stir-fried for 2–3 minutes to reach tenderness.
3. Tip the vegetables to the side of the pan and pour the beaten eggs into the empty space on the other side. The eggs should be thoroughly cooked after being scrambled.
4. Stir-fry the mixture for 3 to 4 minutes, breaking up any rice clumps, then add the cold, cooked Einkorn rice to the pan.
5. After cooking for 1–2 minutes, stir in the soy sauce and sesame oil (if using).
6. If preferred, top the fried rice with thinly sliced green onions.

Einkorn Pad Thai:

Ingredients:

- 8 ounces Einkorn noodles or rice noodles
- Two tablespoons of vegetable oil
- 1 pound shrimp, chicken, or tofu (optional)
- Two cloves garlic, minced
- Two eggs, beaten
- 1 cup bean sprouts
- 1/2 cup chopped peanuts
- Lime wedges for garnish (optional)

For the Pad Thai Sauce:

- 1/4 cup fish sauce (or soy sauce for a vegetarian option)
- Two tablespoons tamarind paste
- Two tablespoons brown sugar
- One tablespoon of rice vinegar

Instructions:

1. Prepare the Einkorn noodles following the directions on the package, drain, and set aside.
2. Combine the fish sauce (or soy sauce), tamarind paste, brown sugar, and rice vinegar in a separate bowl to make the Pad Thai sauce. Place aside.
3. Heat the vegetable oil to a medium-high temperature in a sizable skillet or wok. Cook any shrimp, chicken, or tofu you're using until it's browned and done. Take out of the pan and place aside.
4. Add the minced garlic to the same skillet and cook until fragrant, about 30 seconds.
5. Pour the beaten eggs into the other half of the pan while pushing the garlic to one side. The eggs should be thoroughly cooked after being scrambled.

6. Add the Pad Thai sauce, cooked protein (if using), and Einkorn noodles to the pan. Stir-fry everything for two to three minutes or until thoroughly heated.
7. Cook the bean sprouts for 1-2 minutes after stirring them in.
8. If desired, garnish the Pad Thai with lime wedges and chopped peanuts.

Einkorn Beef and Mushroom Risotto:

Ingredients:

- 1 cup Einkorn rice
- 1/2 pound beef sirloin, thinly sliced
- 1 cup mushrooms, sliced
- 1/2 cup diced onion
- Two cloves garlic, minced
- 4 cups beef broth, heated
- 1/2 cup dry white wine
- Two tablespoons butter
- 1/4 cup grated Parmesan cheese
- Salt and pepper to taste
- Fresh parsley for garnish (optional)

Instructions:

1. Melt the butter in a sizable skillet or pot over medium heat. Add the minced garlic and onion, and cook for two to three minutes or until soft.
2. Include the meat slices and mushrooms in the pan. Cook the beef and mushrooms for 3 to 4 minutes or until the steak is browned. The steak and mushrooms should be taken out of the pan and kept aside.
3. Place the Einkorn rice in the same skillet and toast it for a few minutes while stirring regularly.

4. Add the white wine and boil the rice until it has absorbed most of it.
5. Start by adding a ladleful of the hot beef broth at a time, stirring constantly and waiting for each ladleful to absorb before adding more.
6. Keep doing this for 20 to 25 minutes or until the rice is creamy and soft.
7. Add the meat and mushrooms that have been cooked, the Parmesan cheese that has been grated, and salt and pepper to taste.
8. If wanted, garnish with fresh parsley and serve hot.

Einkorn Spinach and Mushroom Risotto:

Ingredients:

- 1 cup Einkorn rice
- 1 cup mushrooms, sliced
- 1/2 cup diced onion
- Two cloves garlic, minced
- 4 cups vegetable broth, heated
- 1/2 cup dry white wine
- Two tablespoons butter
- 1/4 cup grated Parmesan cheese
- Salt and pepper to taste
- Fresh spinach leaves for garnish (optional)

Instructions:

1. Melt the butter in a sizable skillet or pot over medium heat. Add the minced garlic and onion, and cook for two to three minutes or until soft.
2. Include the mushroom slices in the pan. The mushrooms should be cooked for 3–4 minutes or until soft. Take them out of the pan and place them aside.

3. Place the Einkorn rice in the same skillet and toast it for a few minutes while stirring regularly.
4. Add the white wine and boil the rice until it has absorbed most of it.
5. Start by adding a ladleful of the hot vegetable broth at a time, stirring constantly and waiting for each ladleful to absorb before adding more.
6. Keep doing this for 20 to 25 minutes or until the rice is creamy and soft.
7. Add cooked mushrooms, Parmesan cheese that has been grated, and salt and pepper to taste.
8. If wanted, garnish with fresh spinach leaves and serve hot.

Einkorn Shrimp Scampi:

Ingredients:

- 8 ounces Einkorn spaghetti or linguine
- 1 pound large shrimp, peeled and deveined
- Four cloves garlic, minced
- 1/4 cup white wine
- 1/4 cup fresh lemon juice
- Zest of 1 lemon
- 2 tablespoons unsalted butter
- 2 tablespoons olive oil
- Salt and black pepper to taste
- Chopped fresh parsley for garnish (optional)

Instructions:

1. Prepare the Einkorn spaghetti or linguine per the package's directions. Drain, then set apart.
2. Heat the butter and olive oil in a large skillet over medium-high heat.

3. Add the minced garlic to the skillet and cook until fragrant, about 1 minute.
4. Add the shrimp to the skillet and cook on each side for 1 to 2 minutes or until pink.
5. Please take out the shrimp from the pan and place them aside.
6. Fill the skillet with the white wine, lemon juice, and lemon zest. Bring to a simmer and cook for two to three minutes to slightly decrease.
7. Add the cooked shrimp to the skillet and swirl to evenly distribute the sauce.
8. To taste, add salt and black pepper.
9. Put the cooked Einkorn spaghetti or linguine on top of the shrimp scampi. If desired, garnish with finely chopped fresh parsley.

Einkorn Lemon Garlic Shrimp:

Ingredients:

- 1 pound large shrimp, peeled and deveined
- Four cloves garlic, minced
- Zest and juice of 1 lemon
- 2 tablespoons olive oil
- Two tablespoons chopped fresh parsley
- Salt and black pepper to taste
- Cooked Einkorn rice or pasta for serving

Instructions:

1. In a bowl, combine the minced garlic, lemon zest, olive oil, fresh parsley that has been chopped, salt, and pepper.
2. Place the shrimp in the bowl, peeling and deveining them first. Toss to evenly distribute the marinade. Give them at least 15 minutes to marinate.

3. Turn up the heat to medium-high in a sizable skillet. Add and fry the shrimp for two to three minutes on each side when the shrimp are pink and opaque.
4. Arrange the cooked Einkorn rice or pasta on top of the lemon-garlic shrimp.

Einkorn Baked Salmon:

Ingredients:

- Four salmon fillets
- Two tablespoons of olive oil
- Two cloves garlic, minced
- One lemon, thinly sliced
- One tablespoon of fresh dill, chopped
- Salt and black pepper to taste
- Lemon wedges for garnish (optional)

Instructions:

1. Set the oven's temperature to 375°F (190°C).
2. Arrange the salmon fillets on a baking pan covered with foil or parchment.
3. Drizzle olive oil over the salmon fillets and season with salt, black pepper, minced garlic, and fresh dill.
4. Top each salmon fillet with a slice of lemon.
5. Bake in the oven for 12 to 15 minutes or until the salmon is cooked to your preferred doneness and flakes readily with a fork.
6. If you want, serve the baked salmon with lemon wedges.

Einkorn Grilled Swordfish:

Ingredients:

- Four swordfish steaks
- 2 tablespoons olive oil
- Two cloves garlic, minced
- One lemon, juiced
- One teaspoon dried oregano
- Salt and black pepper to taste
- Lemon wedges for garnish (optional)

Instructions:

1. Set the grill to a medium-high temperature.
2. Combine the salt, black pepper, dried oregano, lemon juice, olive oil, and minced garlic in a bowl.
3. Apply the marinade on both sides of the swordfish steaks.
4. Grill the swordfish steaks on each side for 3 to 4 minutes or until thoroughly cooked.
5. If wanted, serve the grilled swordfish with lemon wedges.

Einkorn Tuna Steak with Chimichurri:

Ingredients: *For the Tuna Steak:*

- 4 tuna steaks
- 2 tablespoons olive oil
- 2 cloves garlic, minced
- Salt and black pepper to taste

For the Chimichurri Sauce:

- 1 cup fresh parsley leaves, chopped
- 1/4 cup fresh cilantro leaves, chopped
- 2 cloves garlic, minced
- 1/4 cup red wine vinegar
- 1/2 cup extra-virgin olive oil
- 1 teaspoon crushed red pepper flakes (adjust to taste)
- Salt and black pepper to taste

Instructions: *For the Tuna Steak:*

1. Combine the olive oil, crushed garlic, salt, and pepper in a bowl.
2. Apply the marinade on both sides of the tuna steaks.
3. Turn up the heat on a grill or grill pan.
4. To cook the tuna steaks rare, grill them for two to three minutes on each side.

For the Chimichurri Sauce:

1. Combine the minced garlic, extra virgin olive oil, red wine vinegar, chopped fresh parsley, chopped fresh cilantro, salt, and black pepper in a bowl. To blend, stir.
2. Drizzle enough Chimichurri sauce over the tuna steaks before serving.

Einkorn Pesto Pasta:

Ingredients:

- 8 ounces Einkorn pasta
- 2 cups fresh basil leaves
- 1/2 cup grated Parmesan cheese

- 1/2 cup pine nuts
- Two cloves garlic, minced
- 1/2 cup extra-virgin olive oil
- Salt and black pepper to taste
- Grated Parmesan cheese for garnish (optional)

Instructions:

1. Prepare the Einkorn pasta in accordance with the directions on the package. Drain, then set apart.
2. Place the fresh basil leaves, grated Parmesan cheese, pine nuts, garlic powder, salt, and black pepper in a food processor.
3. Pulse a few times to blend the ingredients and create a paste.
4. Add the extra virgin olive oil in a slow stream while the food processor runs to create a smooth, well-combined pesto.
5. Combine the pesto sauce with the cooked pasta.
6. If preferred, top the pesto pasta dish with freshly grated Parmesan cheese.

Einkorn Pasta:

Ingredients:

- 1 cup Einkorn flour
- 1 large egg
- 1/2 teaspoon salt
- Water (as needed)

Instructions:

1. Make a well in the center of a mound of Einkorn flour on a smooth surface.
2. Break an egg into the well and sprinkle salt on top.

3. Gently whisk the egg with a fork while introducing the flour gradually from the well's edges. Once the dough begins to come together, continue mixing.
4. Use your hands to knead the dough into a smooth, cohesive ball after it becomes too firm to combine with a fork. You can add a bit of water, one teaspoon at a time, to the dough if it is too dry until it has the right consistency.
5. Cover the dough with plastic wrap and let it rest at room temperature for 30 minutes. This enables the flour to hydrate thoroughly.
6. After the dough has rested, stretch it out with a rolling pin or a pasta machine until it is thin and silky. If it sticks to the surface, sprinkle a little flour over it.
7. Cut the pasta into the fettuccine or spaghetti shapes that you choose.
8. Bring lots of salted water to a boil in a big pot. The Einkorn pasta should be cooked for 2 to 3 minutes or until al dente.
9. After draining the pasta, top it with your preferred sauce.

Einkorn Carbonara:

Ingredients:

- 8 oz Einkorn spaghetti
- 2 large eggs
- 1 cup grated Pecorino Romano cheese
- 4 oz pancetta or guanciale, diced
- 2 cloves garlic, minced
- Salt and black pepper to taste
- Fresh parsley, chopped (for garnish)

Instructions:

1. Boil salted water in a big saucepan until the Einkorn spaghetti is al dente. After draining the pasta, save 1/2 cup of the cooking water.
2. Whisk the eggs and grated Pecorino Romano cheese in another dish while the pasta is cooking. Use black pepper to season.
3. Crisp up the diced pancetta or guanciale in a skillet. Cook for an additional minute after adding the garlic, minced.
4. Turn off the heat under the skillet. Toss the pancetta, garlic, and cooked spaghetti together quickly.
5. Add the pasta to the egg and cheese mixture and toss to incorporate. If the sauce is too thick, thin it out by adding a little of the conserved pasta cooking water.
6. Top with fresh parsley that has been cut, and serve right away.

Einkorn Spaghetti Bolognese:

Ingredients:

- 8 oz Einkorn spaghetti
- 1 lb ground beef
- One onion, finely chopped
- Two cloves garlic, minced
- One carrot, finely diced
- One celery stalk, finely diced
- One can (28 oz) crushed tomatoes
- 1/2 cup red wine (optional)
- One teaspoon dried oregano
- Salt and black pepper to taste
- Grated Parmesan cheese (for serving)

Instructions:

1. Brown the ground beef in a big skillet over medium heat until it's no longer pink. As it cooks, chop it into little pieces. Remove any extra fat.
2. Add the carrot, celery, onion, and garlic to the skillet. Sauté the vegetables for about 5 minutes or until they are tender.
3. Add the smashed tomatoes and, if using, the red wine. Add the salt, black pepper, and dried oregano. The sauce should simmer for 20 to 30 minutes while being occasionally stirred.
4. Cook the Einkorn spaghetti in a big saucepan of salted boiling water until it's al dente while the sauce simmers. Drain.
5. Top the cooked Einkorn noodles with the Bolognese sauce and freshly grated Parmesan cheese.

Einkorn Lasagna:

Ingredients:

- 8 oz Einkorn lasagna noodles
- 1 lb ground beef
- 1 onion, chopped
- 2 cloves garlic, minced
- One can (28 oz) crushed tomatoes
- One can (6 oz) tomato paste
- One teaspoon of dried basil
- 1 teaspoon dried oregano
- Salt and black pepper to taste
- 2 cups ricotta cheese
- One egg
- 2 cups shredded mozzarella cheese
- 1/2 cup grated Parmesan cheese
- Fresh basil leaves (for garnish)

Instructions:

1. Prepare the Einkorn lasagna noodles as directed on the package until they are al dente. Drain, then set apart.
2. Over medium heat, cook the ground beef in a big skillet. Remove any extra fat.
3. Add the minced garlic and onion to the skillet and cook until soft.
4. Add the tomato paste, dried oregano, dry basil, smashed tomatoes, salt, and black pepper. The sauce should simmer for 15 to 20 minutes.
5. Combine the ricotta cheese and egg in another bowl.
6. Set the oven's temperature to 350°F (175°C).
7. Arrange the ingredients in the following order in a 9x13-inch baking dish: a thin layer of sauce, cooked Einkorn lasagna noodles, half of the ricotta mixture, half of the mozzarella cheese, and a sprinkle of Parmesan cheese. Continue stacking in this manner.
8. Bake the baking dish for 25 minutes with the foil covering.
9. Take off the foil and bake for 25 to 30 minutes or until bubbling and brown.
10. Give it some time to rest before serving. Fresh basil leaves are a lovely garnish.

Einkorn Chicken Tacos:

Ingredients:

- 1 lb boneless, skinless chicken breasts cut into strips
- One tablespoon of olive oil
- One onion, chopped
- Two cloves garlic, minced
- One bell pepper, sliced
- One packet of taco seasoning mix
- 8 small Einkorn tortillas

- Toppings: shredded lettuce, diced tomatoes, cheese, sour cream, salsa, etc.

Instructions:

1. Place a large skillet over medium heat and add the olive oil. When aromatic and softened, add the minced onion and garlic.
2. Include the chicken strips and heat them until the pink color has disappeared.
3. Combine the taco spice mix with the bell pepper slices. Cook for a few more minutes or until the chicken is thoroughly seasoned and the peppers are soft.
4. Heat the Einkorn tortillas in a dry skillet or microwave as directed on the package.
5. Assemble your tacos by dividing the chicken mixture among the tortillas and adding your preferred toppings.

Einkorn Beef Enchiladas:

Ingredients:

- 1 lb ground beef
- One small onion, chopped
- Two cloves garlic, minced
- One can (10 oz) red enchilada sauce
- One can (4 oz) diced green chilies
- One teaspoon of ground cumin
- 1/2 teaspoon chili powder
- Salt and black pepper to taste
- 8 small Einkorn tortillas
- 2 cups shredded cheddar cheese
- Sour cream, diced tomatoes, and chopped cilantro (for garnish)

Instructions:

1. Set the oven's temperature to 350°F (175°C).
2. Over medium heat, cook the ground beef in a big skillet. Remove any extra fat.
3. Add the minced garlic and diced onion to the skillet and cook until soft.
4. Add the diced green chilies, ground cumin, chili powder, salt, and black pepper. Also, stir in the red enchilada sauce. For a few minutes, simmer.
5. Divide the beef mixture among the Einkorn tortillas, top with grated cheddar cheese, and roll each tortilla up.
6. Arrange the rolled enchiladas in a baking dish seam-side down.
7. Add extra cheese and drizzle any remaining sauce over the top of the enchiladas.
8. Bake the cheese until it is bubbling and brown, about 20 minutes.
9. Garnish the dish with sour cream, diced tomatoes, and chopped cilantro.

Einkorn Chicken Quesadillas:

Ingredients:

- 2 cups cooked chicken, shredded
- 1 cup shredded cheddar cheese
- 1 cup shredded Monterey Jack cheese
- 1/2 cup diced bell peppers (any color)
- 1/4 cup diced red onion
- 4 large Einkorn tortillas
- Olive oil or cooking spray
- Sour cream, salsa, and guacamole (for dipping)

Instructions:

1. Combine the diced bell peppers, red onion, cheddar cheese, and Monterey Jack cheese in a big bowl. Mix thoroughly.
2. Lay one Einkorn tortilla on a spotless surface, then evenly distribute half with the chicken and cheese mixture.
3. To make a half-moon shape, fold the other half of the tortilla over to cover the filling.
4. Lightly coat a skillet or griddle with cooking spray or olive oil and heat over medium-high heat.
5. Put the quesadilla in the skillet and cook it on each side for two to three minutes, or until the cheese has melted and the tortilla is crunchy.
6. Carry out step 6 using the remaining tortillas and filling.
7. Cut the quesadillas into wedges and provide salsa, guacamole, and sour cream for dipping.

Einkorn Fish Tacos:

Ingredients:

- 1 lb white fish fillets (e.g., cod or tilapia)
- 1 cup Einkorn flour
- One teaspoon paprika
- 1/2 teaspoon garlic powder
- Salt and black pepper to taste
- 1 cup buttermilk
- 8 small Einkorn tortillas
- Shredded cabbage or lettuce
- Sliced tomatoes
- Sliced red onions
- Sliced jalapeños (optional)
- Lime wedges

- Creamy cilantro lime sauce (recipe below)

Instructions:

1. In a shallow basin, combine the Einkorn flour, paprika, garlic powder, salt, and black pepper.
2. Buttermilk should be used to dip each fish fillet before being coated in the seasoned flour mixture.
3. In a skillet, heat the oil over medium-high heat. Fry the coated fish fillets on each side for 3–4 minutes or until they are crisp and golden. On paper towels, drain.
4. A microwave or a dry skillet can be used to reheat Einkorn tortillas.
5. To assemble the fish tacos, put a piece of fried fish in each tortilla and top with lettuce or cabbage shreds, tomatoes, red onions, and if preferred, jalapenos.
6. Include a creamy cilantro lime sauce and lime wedges with your meal.

Creamy Cilantro Lime Sauce:

Ingredients:

- 1/2 cup mayonnaise
- 1/2 cup sour cream
- 1/4 cup fresh cilantro, chopped
- Two tablespoons of lime juice
- 1 teaspoon lime zest
- One clove of garlic, minced
- Salt and black pepper to taste

Instructions:

1. Combine mayonnaise, sour cream, cilantro, lime juice, zest, finely minced garlic, salt, and black pepper in a bowl.
2. Place the flavors in the refrigerator at least 30 minutes before serving to enable the flavors to mingle.

Einkorn Vegetarian Burritos:

Ingredients:

- 1 cup cooked Einkorn rice
- One can (15 oz) black beans, drained and rinsed
- 1 cup diced tomatoes
- 1 cup diced bell peppers (any color)
- 1 cup corn kernels (fresh, frozen, or canned)
- One teaspoon of ground cumin
- 1/2 teaspoon chili powder
- Salt and black pepper to taste
- 8 large Einkorn tortillas
- Shredded cheese (optional)
- Sour cream, salsa, and guacamole (for serving)

Instructions:

1. Combine the cooked Einkorn rice, black beans, diced tomatoes, bell peppers, and corn in a big skillet.
2. Add salt, black pepper, chili powder, ground cumin, and other seasonings. Cook until thoroughly cooked and well blended over medium heat.
3. A microwave or a dry skillet can be used to reheat Einkorn tortillas.
4. Divide the rice and bean mixture among the tortillas. Add some shredded cheese if you like.
5. To make a burrito, fold the tortilla's sides in and roll it up.
6. Top with salsa, guacamole, and sour cream.

Einkorn Beef Fajitas:

Ingredients:

- 1 lb thinly sliced beef (such as flank steak or skirt steak)
- Two tablespoons of olive oil
- One onion, sliced
- 1 bell pepper, sliced
- One teaspoon of chili powder
- One teaspoon of ground cumin
- 1/2 teaspoon paprika
- Salt and black pepper to taste
- 8 small Einkorn tortillas
- Salsa, guacamole, and sour cream (for serving)

Instructions:

1. Heat the olive oil in a large skillet over medium-high heat.
2. Add the beef that has been thinly sliced to the skillet and cook for a few minutes or until it is browned and cooked to the desired doneness. Could you remove the beef from the skillet and set it aside?
3. Include the bell pepper and onion slices in the same skillet. Sauté until they are soft and just beginning to caramelize.
4. Add the steak back to the skillet along with the peppers and onions.
5. Add salt, black pepper, paprika, cumin powder, and chili powder to the mixture as seasonings. Cook for a few more minutes or until the mixture is well heated.
6. A microwave or a dry skillet can be used to reheat Einkorn tortillas.
7. Arrange the warmed tortillas with the beef fajita mixture on top, and serve with salsa, guacamole, and sour cream on the side.

Einkorn Chicken Quesadillas:

Ingredients:

- 2 cups cooked chicken, shredded
- 1 cup shredded cheddar cheese
- 1 cup shredded Monterey Jack cheese
- 1/2 cup diced bell peppers (any color)
- 1/4 cup diced red onion
- 4 large Einkorn tortillas
- Olive oil or cooking spray
- Sour cream, salsa, and guacamole (for dipping)

Instructions:

1. Combine the diced bell peppers, red onion, cheddar cheese, and Monterey Jack cheese in a big bowl. Mix thoroughly.
2. Lay one Einkorn tortilla on a spotless surface, then evenly distribute half of it with the chicken and cheese mixture.
3. To make a half-moon shape, fold the other half of the tortilla over to cover the filling.
4. Lightly coat a skillet or griddle with cooking spray or olive oil and heat over medium-high heat.
5. Put the quesadilla in the skillet and cook it on each side for two to three minutes, or until the cheese has melted and the tortilla is crunchy.
6. Carry out step 6 using the remaining tortillas and filling.
7. Cut the quesadillas into wedges and provide salsa, guacamole, and sour cream for dipping.

Einkorn Beef and Broccoli Noodles:

Ingredients:

- 8 oz Einkorn noodles
- 1 lb beef sirloin, thinly sliced
- 2 cups broccoli florets
- 1/4 cup soy sauce
- 2 tablespoons oyster sauce
- Two cloves garlic, minced
- Two tablespoons of vegetable oil
- One teaspoon cornstarch
- Sesame seeds (for garnish, optional)

Instructions:

1. Prepare the Einkorn noodles as directed on the package until they are al dente. Drain, then set apart.
2. Combine the soy sauce, oyster sauce, cornstarch, and minced garlic in a small bowl. Place aside.
3. Heat one tablespoon of vegetable oil over high heat in a big skillet or wok. The meat should be stir-fried until it is well-browned and cooked to your preference. Could you remove the beef from the skillet and set it aside?
4. Add the final tablespoon of vegetable oil to the same skillet. The broccoli florets should be stir-fried for 3–4 minutes or until crisp-tender.
5. Add the cooked Einkorn noodles to the skillet along with the cooked beef.
6. Drizzle the steak, noodles, and broccoli with the sauce mixture—Stir-fry for 2 to 3 minutes or until everything is thoroughly cooked and coated.
7. If preferred, garnish with sesame seeds before serving.

Einkorn Sweet and Sour Chicken:

Ingredients:

- 1 lb boneless, skinless chicken breasts cut into bite-sized pieces
- 1 cup Einkorn flour
- Salt and black pepper to taste
- Vegetable oil for frying
- One bell pepper, diced
- One onion, diced
- One can (8 oz) pineapple chunks, drained
- 1/2 cup sweet and sour sauce (store-bought or homemade)

Instructions:

1. Add salt and black pepper to the chicken pieces.
2. Put the Einkorn flour in a bowl that is just a little deep. Chicken pieces should be dredged in flour, with excess flour to be shaken off.
3. Heat vegetable oil over medium-high heat in a large skillet or frying pan. Cook the coated chicken pieces through and until they are golden brown. Remove, then dry off with paper towels.
4. Saute the diced bell pepper and onion in a separate skillet until tender.
5. Include the cooked chicken and the chunks of drained pineapple in the pan.
6. Cover the chicken, peppers, and pineapple with the sweet-sour sauce. Stir to distribute the coating evenly.
7. Continue cooking for an additional 2 to 3 minutes to thoroughly reheat.
8. Put cooked Einkorn rice on the plate.

Einkorn General Tso's Chicken:

Ingredients:

- 1 lb boneless, skinless chicken thighs cut into bite-sized pieces
- 1 cup Einkorn flour
- Salt and black pepper to taste
- Vegetable oil for frying
- 1/4 cup soy sauce
- Two tablespoons of hoisin sauce
- Two tablespoons of rice vinegar
- 2 tablespoons brown sugar
- Two cloves garlic, minced
- One teaspoon of fresh ginger, grated
- 1/2 teaspoon red pepper flakes (adjust to taste)
- Sliced green onions (for garnish)
- Cooked Einkorn rice (for serving)

Instructions:

1. Add salt and black pepper to the chicken pieces.
2. Put the Einkorn flour in a bowl that is just a little deep. Chicken pieces should be dredged in flour, with excess flour to be shaken off.
3. Heat vegetable oil over medium-high heat in a large skillet or frying pan. Cook the coated chicken pieces through and until they are golden brown. Remove, then dry off with paper towels.
4. Combine the soy sauce, hoisin sauce, rice vinegar, brown sugar, chopped garlic, grated ginger, and red pepper flakes in a separate saucepan. Stirring frequently; heat over medium heat for 2 to 3 minutes or until the sauce thickens.
5. Cover the cooked chicken pieces with the sauce by pouring it over them.

6. Top with chopped green onions and serve over Einkorn rice that has been cooked.

Einkorn Orange Chicken:

Ingredients:

- 1 lb boneless, skinless chicken breasts cut into bite-sized pieces
- 1 cup Einkorn flour
- Salt and black pepper to taste
- Vegetable oil for frying
- 1/4 cup orange juice
- Zest of 1 orange
- 1/4 cup soy sauce
- Two tablespoons brown sugar
- Two cloves garlic, minced
- 1/2 teaspoon ginger, grated
- 1/4 teaspoon red pepper flakes (adjust to taste)
- Sliced green onions and sesame seeds (for garnish)
- Cooked Einkorn rice (for serving)

Instructions:

1. Add salt and black pepper to the chicken pieces.
2. Put the Einkorn flour in a bowl that is just a little deep. Chicken pieces should be dredged in flour, with excess flour to be shaken off.
3. Heat vegetable oil over medium-high heat in a large skillet or frying pan. Cook the coated chicken pieces through and until they are golden brown. Remove, then dry off with paper towels.
4. Combine orange juice, orange zest, soy sauce, brown sugar, chopped ginger, red pepper flakes, and soy sauce

in a skillet. Simmer for 2 to 3 minutes over medium heat to thicken the sauce.

5. Cover the cooked chicken pieces with the orange sauce by pouring it over them.
6. Arrange sliced green onions and sesame seeds on top of cooked Einkorn rice before serving.

Einkorn Chicken Alfredo:

Ingredients:

- 8 oz Einkorn fettuccine pasta
- Two boneless, skinless chicken breasts cut into bite-sized pieces
- Two tablespoons of olive oil
- Two cloves garlic, minced
- 1 cup heavy cream
- 1/2 cup grated Parmesan cheese
- Salt and black pepper to taste
- Fresh parsley, chopped (for garnish)

Instructions:

1. Prepare the Einkorn fettuccine pasta as directed on the package until it is al dente. Drain, then set apart.
2. Heat the olive oil in a large skillet over medium-high heat. Add the chicken pieces and sauté them until their exterior is golden brown and the interior is no longer pink. The chicken should be taken out of the skillet and put aside.
3. Add minced garlic to the same skillet and cook until fragrant, about 1 minute.
4. Add the heavy cream and boil the mixture. Turn down the heat and cook for two to three minutes or until it slightly thickens.

5. Season the sauce with salt and black pepper after incorporating the grated Parmesan cheese. Till the cheese has melted and the sauce is creamy, simmer while stirring.
6. Add the cooked chicken back to the skillet and heat it through for a couple more minutes.
7. Top the cooked Einkorn fettuccine with the Alfredo sauce and fresh parsley that has been chopped.

Einkorn Beef and Pepper Stir-Fry:

Ingredients:

- 1 lb flank steak, thinly sliced against the grain
- 2 tablespoons soy sauce
- 2 tablespoons oyster sauce
- One tablespoon cornstarch
- 1/2 teaspoon sugar
- Two tablespoons of vegetable oil
- 1 red bell pepper, thinly sliced
- One green bell pepper, thinly sliced
- One onion, thinly sliced
- Two cloves garlic, minced
- Salt and black pepper to taste
- Cooked Einkorn rice (for serving)

Instructions:

1. Mix the soy, oyster, cornstarch, and sugar in a bowl. Add the flank steak that has been thinly sliced and marinade for about 15 minutes.
2. Heat one tablespoon of vegetable oil over high heat in a wok or sizable skillet. The marinated beef should be stir-fried until it is well-browned and done. It is taken out of the wok and placed aside.

3. Fill the wok with the final tablespoon of vegetable oil. Add the minced garlic, thinly sliced onion, and chopped red and green bell peppers. Stir-fry the vegetables until they are crisp-tender.
4. Add salt and black pepper to the cooked beef before adding it back to the wok.
5. Place the cooked Einkorn rice on top of the meat and pepper stir-fry.

Einkorn Pork Fried Rice:

Ingredients:

- 2 cups cooked Einkorn rice, cold (day-old rice works best)
- 1/2 lb pork loin or pork chops, diced
- Two tablespoons of vegetable oil
- 1/2 cup frozen peas and carrots, thawed
- Two cloves garlic, minced
- Two tablespoons of soy sauce
- 1/2 teaspoon sesame oil
- Two green onions, chopped
- Two eggs, beaten
- Salt and black pepper to taste

Instructions:

1. Heat one tablespoon of vegetable oil over high heat in a big skillet or wok. Stir-fry the pork cubes after adding them until they are thoroughly done and beginning to color. Could you remove the pork from the skillet and set it aside?
2. Add the final tablespoon of vegetable oil to the same skillet—Stir-fry the minced garlic for about 30 seconds or until fragrant.

3. Pour the beaten eggs into the opposite half of the skillet while pushing the garlic to one side. The eggs should be scrambled until they are done but slightly wet.
4. Include the cooked Einkorn rice and stir-fry it for a couple of minutes to reheat it.
5. Include the cooked pork, thawed peas and carrots, soy sauce, and sesame oil. Stir-fry the ingredients until they are hot and well combined.
6. To taste, add salt and black pepper to the fried rice.
7. Turn off the heat, add some finely chopped green onions, and serve.

Einkorn BBQ Pulled Pork Sandwich:

Ingredients:

- 2 lbs boneless pork shoulder or pork butt
- 1 cup BBQ sauce (your choice)
- One onion, sliced
- 1/2 cup chicken broth
- One teaspoon of garlic powder
- One teaspoon paprika
- Salt and black pepper to taste
- Hamburger buns or sandwich rolls
- Coleslaw (optional for topping)

Instructions:

1. Use salt, black pepper, garlic powder, paprika, and other seasonings to season the pork shoulder or pig butt.
2. Fill the bottom of a slow cooker with onion slices. On top of the onions, position the seasoned pork.
3. Cover the meat with the BBQ sauce and chicken broth.

4. Cook the pork on low for 6 to 8 hours or until it is soft and can be easily torn with a fork.
5. Remove the pork from the slow cooker using two forks and shred it.
6. Add the sauce and onions to the slow cooker with the shredded pork.
7. Place the BBQ pulled pork on burger buns or sandwich rolls and, if preferred, cover with coleslaw.

Einkorn Beef Brisket:

Ingredients:

- 3-4 lbs beef brisket
- Two tablespoons of vegetable oil
- 1 onion, sliced
- Four cloves garlic, minced
- 1 cup beef broth
- 1 cup BBQ sauce
- Salt and black pepper to taste

Instructions:

1. Add black pepper and salt to the beef brisket.
2. Heat the vegetable oil over medium-high heat in a big skillet or Dutch oven. The brisket should be golden on both sides after being seared. The brisket should be taken out of the skillet and put aside.
3. Add the minced garlic and onion slices to the same skillet. Sauté the onion until it turns translucent.
4. Reintroduce the seared brisket to the pan. Beef broth and BBQ sauce should be added.
5. Cover the skillet with a cover or move everything into a roasting pan.
6. Bake the brisket for 3–4 hours at 325°F (160°C) or until it is cooked and quickly shreds with a fork.

7. Take the beef out of the oven, give it some time to rest, and then slice or shred it.
8. If preferred, top the food with more barbecue sauce.

Einkorn Smoked Ribs:

Ingredients:
- Pork ribs
- Einkorn flour for a dusting
- Your favorite BBQ rub or sauce
- Wood chips for smoking

Instructions:
1. Use your preferred BBQ sauce or rub to season the pork ribs.
2. To form a thin layer, sprinkle Einkorn flour over the ribs.
3. With wood chips for smoking, preheat your smoker to the required temperature, often around 225°F or 107°C.
4. Smoke the ribs for several hours until they are juicy and flavorful from the smoke. As required, baste with extra barbecue sauce.

Einkorn Meatloaf:

Ingredients:
- Ground beef or a mixture of beef and pork
- Einkorn breadcrumbs
- Chopped onions, celery, and carrots
- Eggs
- Salt, pepper, and your choice of seasonings
- Ketchup or tomato sauce for topping

Instructions:

1. Combine the ground beef, Einkorn breadcrumbs, finely chopped veggies, eggs, and seasonings in a bowl.
2. Create a loaf from the mixture and set it in a baking dish.
3. Drizzle tomato sauce or ketchup on top.
4. Bake for about an hour, or until thoroughly cooked, in an oven warmed to 350°F (175°C).

Einkorn Beef Tacos:

Ingredients:

- Ground beef
- Einkorn flour tortillas
- Taco seasoning
- Shredded lettuce, diced tomatoes, shredded cheese, sour cream, and salsa for toppings

Instructions:

1. According to the directions on the taco seasoning packet, brown the ground beef in a skillet with the seasoning.
2. A microwave or a dry skillet can be used to reheat Einkorn wheat tortillas.
3. Arrange your preferred toppings on top of the tortillas with the seasoned beef.

Einkorn Chili Cheese Dogs:

Ingredients:

- Hot dogs
- Einkorn hot dog buns
- Chili (homemade or canned)

- Shredded cheddar cheese
- Diced onions and jalapeños (optional)

Instructions:

1. Prepare the hot dogs whichever you like (grill, boil, pan-fry).
2. Reheat the Einkorn dog buns.
3. Place a cooked hot dog, chili, cheddar cheese shavings, optional onions, and jalapenos on top of each bun.

Einkorn Sloppy Joes:

Ingredients:

- Ground beef
- Einkorn hamburger buns
- Onion, bell pepper (chopped)
- Tomato sauce
- Brown sugar, Worcestershire sauce, and spices for seasoning

Instructions:

1. Brown the ground beef in a skillet while adding chopped bell peppers and onions.
2. Remove any extra fat, then add Worcestershire sauce, brown sugar, and spices to taste.
3. Simmer the mixture until it becomes thick.
4. Put the hamburgers on Einkorn bread.

Einkorn Beef Stroganoff:

Ingredients:

- Beef strips or cubes
- Einkorn egg noodles or rice
- Mushrooms, onions (sliced)
- Sour cream
- Beef broth
- Flour for dredging
- Butter or oil for cooking
- Salt and pepper

Instructions:

1. Using butter or oil in a skillet, brown the meat after dredging it in flour.
2. Remove the steak from the pan, then sauté the mushrooms and onions.
3. To create a creamy sauce, combine beef broth and sour cream.
4. Add the steak back to the skillet and cook it thoroughly.
5. Serve with rice or Einkorn egg noodles.

Einkorn Beef and Guinness Stew:

Ingredients:

- Stewing beef
- Einkorn flour for dredging
- Onions, carrots, and potatoes (chopped)
- Guinness stout or other stout beer
- Beef broth
- Herbs and spices (such as thyme and bay leaves)
- Butter or oil for cooking
- Salt and pepper

Instructions:

1. Coat the steak with Einkorn flour before browning it with butter or oil in a big pot.
2. Take the meat from the pan and cook the potatoes, onions, and carrots until they soften.
3. Add Guinness, beef broth, herbs, and spices to the saucepan with the beef.
4. Simmer the stew on low heat until it has thickened and the beef is cooked.

Einkorn Lamb Chops:

Ingredients:

- Lamb chops
- Einkorn breadcrumbs
- Olive oil
- Garlic, rosemary, and thyme (minced)
- Salt and pepper

Instructions:

1. On the lamb chops, sprinkle salt, pepper, minced garlic, rosemary, thyme, and Einkorn breadcrumbs.
2. In a skillet with hot olive oil, saute the lamb chops until they are cooked to your preference.

Einkorn Gyros:

Ingredients:

- Thinly sliced beef or lamb
- Einkorn pita bread
- Tzatziki sauce (see recipe below)
- Sliced tomatoes, onions, and lettuce
- Optional toppings like feta cheese and olives

Instructions:

1. Cook the thinly sliced meat on a grill or in a pan.
2. Warm pita made from Einkorn.
3. Assemble the gyros by layering the cooked meat, tomatoes, onions, lettuce, and a liberal amount of tzatziki sauce on top of the pita bread.

Einkorn Beef Kebabs:

Ingredients:

- Cubed beef
- Einkorn flour for dusting (optional)
- Marinade (olive oil, lemon juice, garlic, and your choice of spices)
- Skewers (wooden or metal)

Instructions:

1. For at least an hour, marinate the beef cubes in the marinade.
2. Skewers with marinated beef should be used.
3. Broil or grill the kebabs until they are done to your preference.

Einkorn Chicken Shawarma:

Ingredients:

- Chicken thighs or breasts (sliced)
- Shawarma marinade (yogurt, lemon juice, garlic, and spices)
- Einkorn flatbreads
- Tzatziki sauce (see recipe below)
- Sliced tomatoes, cucumbers, and onions

Instructions:

1. For at least an hour, marinate the chicken in the shawarma marinade.
2. Finish cooking the chicken on a grill or in a pan.
3. Arrange the tzatziki sauce, tomatoes, cucumbers, onions, and chicken atop Einkorn flatbreads.

Einkorn Falafel:

Ingredients:

- Chickpeas (canned or cooked)
- Einkorn flour
- Onion, garlic, and fresh herbs (such as parsley and cilantro)
- Spices (cumin, coriander, paprika)
- Baking powder
- Salt and pepper
- Oil for frying

Instructions:

1. In a food processor, combine chickpeas, Einkorn flour, minced onion, garlic, herbs, spices, baking powder, salt, and pepper.
2. Continue processing until the mixture is well-combined and smooth.
3. Create little patties or balls out of the ingredients.
4. Fry the falafel in hot oil until they are golden brown all around.
5. Present vegetables and tahini sauce with pita bread.

Einkorn Spanakopita:

Ingredients:

- Einkorn phyllo pastry sheets
- Spinach, cooked and drained
- Feta cheese
- Eggs
- Onion and garlic (sautéed)
- Olive oil
- Salt and pepper

Instructions:

1. Combine the cooked spinach, feta cheese crumbles, sautéed onion and garlic, beaten eggs, olive oil, salt, and pepper in a bowl.
2. Arrange sheets of Einkorn phyllo pastry on a baking dish, each with a thin layer of olive oil.
3. Evenly distribute the spinach-feta mixture between the layers.
4. Add one more layer of pastry sheets and brush them all with oil.
5. Bake the pastry until it turns golden, and the filling is firm.

Einkorn Moussaka:

Ingredients:

- Ground beef or lamb
- Einkorn flour for a roux
- Eggplant, sliced and roasted
- Bechamel sauce
- Tomato sauce
- Onion, garlic, and spices (cinnamon, nutmeg)
- Olive oil

- Salt and pepper

1. Brown the ground meat with the seasonings, onion, and garlic.
2. Stir in the tomato sauce.
3. Mix milk into an Einkorn flour and olive oil roux

to make a bechamel sauce.

4. Arrange roasted eggplant, meat sauce, and bechamel in a baking dish.
5. Bake till bubbling and brown.

Einkorn Tzatziki Sauce:

Ingredients:

- Greek yogurt
- Cucumber, grated and drained
- Garlic, minced
- Lemon juice
- Fresh dill or mint (optional)
- Salt and pepper

Instructions:

1. Combine Greek yogurt, finely grated cucumber, minced garlic, lemon juice, and any additional fresh herbs in a bowl.
2. To taste, add salt and pepper to the food.
3. Before serving, place in the fridge for at least one hour.

Einkorn Baklava:

Ingredients:

- Einkorn phyllo pastry sheets
- Nuts (usually a mixture of walnuts, almonds, or pistachios), finely chopped
- Butter, melted
- Ground cinnamon
- Sugar
- Syrup (sugar, water, honey, lemon juice, and orange blossom or rosewater)

Instructions:

1. Set the oven's temperature to 350°F (175°C).
2. Combine the sugar, cinnamon, and nuts that have been finely chopped in a bowl.
3. Spread melted butter in a baking dish, then layer sheets of Einkorn phyllo crust, adding additional butter.
4. Cover the phyllo sheets with a layer of the nut mixture.
5. Continue layering phyllo sheets and nuts until all of the nuts are used, then add a final phyllo layer on top.
6. Slice the baklava into square or diamond-shaped pieces using a sharp knife.
7. Bake in the oven for 45 to 50 minutes or until golden brown.
8. Boil the syrup ingredients—sugar, water, honey, lemon juice, and flavorings—until it slightly thickens while the baklava bakes.
9. When the baklava is done, drizzle the hot syrup over it. Before serving, let it cool.

Einkorn Rice Pudding:

Ingredients:

- Einkorn rice
- Milk
- Sugar
- Vanilla extract
- Cinnamon (for garnish)
- Raisins (optional)

Instructions:

1. Use cold water to rinse the Einkorn rice.
2. Combine the rice, milk, and sugar in a pot.
3. Cook over medium heat, stirring often, for 20 to 30 minutes or until the rice is cooked and the mixture thickens.
4. Add raisins and vanilla extract if using.
5. Turn off the heat and let the food to briefly cool.
6. Garnish the rice pudding with a dusting of cinnamon and serve it warm or cold.

Einkorn Chocolate Cake:

Ingredients:

- 1 1/2 cups einkorn flour
- 1 1/2 cups granulated sugar
- 1/2 cup unsweetened cocoa powder
- 1 1/2 tsp baking powder
- 1 1/2 tsp baking soda
- 1 tsp salt
- 2 eggs
- 1 cup buttermilk
- 1/2 cup vegetable oil
- 2 tsp vanilla extract
- 1 cup boiling water

- For frosting: Use your favorite chocolate frosting recipe.

Instructions:

1. Set the oven's temperature to 350°F (175°C). Prepare two 9-inch round cake pans with oil and flour.
2. Combine einkorn flour, sugar, cocoa powder, baking powder, baking soda, and salt in a sizable basin.
3. Include vanilla essence, buttermilk, eggs, and vegetable oil. Combine thoroughly after mixing.
4. Once the batter is smooth, add hot water and stir. Though thin, that's alright.
5. Evenly distribute the batter among the prepared pans.
6. Bake the cake for 30-35 minutes, or until a toothpick inserted in the middle comes out clean.
7. After the cakes have cooled in the pans for ten minutes, move them to a wire rack to finish cooling.
8. Spread your preferred chocolate frosting on the cakes once they have cooled.

Einkorn Vanilla Cupcakes:

Ingredients:

- 1 1/2 cups einkorn flour
- 1 1/2 tsp baking powder
- 1/2 tsp salt
- 1/2 cup unsalted butter, softened
- 1 cup granulated sugar
- Two large eggs
- 2 tsp vanilla extract
- 1/2 cup whole milk

Instructions:

1. Set the oven's temperature to 350°F (175°C). Cupcake liners should be used to line a muffin pan.

2. Combine baking powder, salt, and einkorn flour in a bowl.
3. In another dish, combine the butter and sugar and beat until frothy.
4. Beat well after each addition of the eggs, one at a time. Add the vanilla extract and stir.
5. Begin and end with the dry ingredients as you gradually add the milk in between additions of the dry components to the wet mixture.
6. Spoon batter into each cupcake liner until it is about two-thirds filled.
7. Bake for 18 to 20 minutes or until a toothpick inserted in the middle of the cake comes out clean.
8. After the cupcakes have finished cooling in the pan for a few minutes, please remove them and let them finish cooling thoroughly before icing.

Einkorn Lemon Bars:

Ingredients:
- 1 1/2 cups einkorn flour
- 1/2 cup powdered sugar
- 1/2 cup unsalted butter, softened
- Four large eggs
- 1 1/2 cups granulated sugar
- 1/4 cup einkorn flour
- Zest and juice of 2 lemons
- Powdered sugar for dusting

Instructions:

1. Set the oven's temperature to 350°F (175°C). A 9x13-inch baking pan should be greased.
2. Mix 1 1/2 cups of einkorn flour, powdered sugar, and softened butter until the mixture resembles coarse crumbs.
3. Place the prepared baking dish on the mixture and bake for 20 minutes.
4. Combine the eggs, granulated sugar, 1/4 cup einkorn flour, lemon juice, and zest while the Crust bakes.
5. After the Crust has baked, spread the lemon mixture over it and put the dish back in the oven for 20 to 25 minutes or until the filling is set.
6. After completely cooling, dust the bars with powdered sugar and cut them into squares.

Einkorn Raspberry Pie:

Ingredients:

- 2 1/2 cups einkorn flour
- 1 tsp salt
- 1 cup unsalted butter, cold and cubed
- 1/2 cup ice water
- 4 cups fresh raspberries
- 1 cup granulated sugar
- 3 tbsp cornstarch
- 1 tbsp lemon juice
- 1 tbsp butter

Instructions:

1. Combine salt and einkorn flour in a big bowl. Until the mixture resembles coarse crumbs, gradually include the cold butter.
2. Continue mixing as you gradually add ice water until the dough comes together. The dough should be divided in half, wrapped in plastic wrap, and chilled for at least an hour.
3. Set the oven's temperature to 425°F (220°C).
4. To fit a 9-inch pie dish, roll out one dough ball on a floured board. Set it inside the dish.
5. Combine raspberries, cornstarch, lemon juice, and granulated sugar in a bowl. Fill the pie crust with the ingredients.
6. Add butter dots to the filling.
7. After rolling it out, spread the second dough ball on top of the filling. To seal the pie, trim and crimp the edges.
8. To let steam out, make a few slits in the top Crust.
9. Bake for 45 to 55 minutes or until the filling is bubbling and the Crust is golden brown.
10. Let the pie cool completely before slicing.

Einkorn Blueberry Cobbler:

Ingredients:

- 4 cups fresh or frozen blueberries
- 1 cup granulated sugar
- 1 cup einkorn flour
- 1 tsp baking powder
- 1/2 tsp salt
- 1 cup milk
- 1/2 cup unsalted butter, melted
- 1 tsp vanilla extract

Instructions:

1. Set the oven's temperature to 350°F (175°C).
2. Combine the blueberries and 1/2 cup of granulated sugar in a mixing basin. Spread them out in a baking dish after tossing them to coat.
3. Combine the einkorn flour, salt, baking soda, and 1/2 cup of sugar in a separate dish.
4. After adding the butter has melted, add the milk and vanilla essence.
5. Cover the blueberries with a uniform layer of batter.
6. Bake for 45 to 50 minutes or until the blueberries pop and the topping is golden brown.
7. Let it cool just a little before serving. If preferred, serve warm with ice cream.

Einkorn Strawberry Shortcake:

Ingredients:

- 1 1/2 cups einkorn flour
- 1/4 cup granulated sugar
- 2 tsp baking powder
- 1/2 tsp salt
- 1/3 cup unsalted butter, cold and cubed
- 1/2 cup whole milk
- 1 tsp vanilla extract
- 2 cups fresh strawberries, sliced
- Whipped cream for topping

Instructions:

1. Set the oven's temperature to 425°F (220°C).
2. Combine einkorn flour, salt, baking soda, and granulated sugar in a bowl.
3. Add the cold butter and stir until it resembles coarse crumbs.

4. Add the vanilla essence and milk, stirring until the dough comes together.
5. To make shortcakes, drop spoonfuls of the dough onto a baking sheet.
6. Bake the potatoes for 10 to 12 minutes or until golden brown.
7. Cut the shortcakes in half; top the bottom halves with strawberries, whipped cream, and the other half of the shortcake.

Einkorn Chocolate Chip Cookies:

Ingredients:

- 1 1/2 cups einkorn flour
- 1/2 tsp baking soda
- 1/2 tsp salt
- 1/2 cup unsalted butter, softened
- 1/2 cup granulated sugar
- 1/2 cup packed brown sugar
- One large egg
- 1 tsp vanilla extract
- 1 cup chocolate chips

Instructions:

1. Set the oven's temperature to 350°F (175°C). Use parchment paper to cover a baking sheet.
2. Combine einkorn flour, baking soda, and salt in a bowl.
3. Combine the softened butter, brown sugar, and granulated sugar in another dish and beat until fluffy.
4. Continue beating after adding the egg and vanilla essence.
5. After gradually adding the dry ingredients, stir the chocolate chips into the wet mixture.

6. Spoon heaping tablespoons of cookie dough onto the preheated baking sheet.
7. Bake for 10 to 12 minutes or until golden brown around the edges.
8. After the cookies have cooled slightly on the baking sheet, move them to a wire rack to finish cooling.

Einkorn Oatmeal Raisin Cookies:

Ingredients:

- 1 1/2 cups einkorn flour
- 1/2 tsp baking soda
- 1/2 tsp salt
- 1/2 cup unsalted butter, softened
- 1/2 cup granulated sugar
- 1/2 cup packed brown sugar
- One large egg
- 1 tsp vanilla extract
- 1 1/2 cups old-fashioned oats
- 1 cup raisins

Instructions:

1. Set the oven's temperature to 350°F (175°C). Use parchment paper to cover a baking sheet.
2. Combine einkorn flour, baking soda, and salt in a bowl.
3. Combine the softened butter, brown sugar, and granulated sugar in another dish and beat until fluffy.
4. Continue beating after adding the egg and vanilla essence.
5. After gradually incorporating the dry ingredients, stir the oats and raisins into the wet mixture.
6. Spoon heaping tablespoons of cookie dough onto the preheated baking sheet.

7. Bake for 10 to 12 minutes or until golden brown around the edges.
8. After the cookies have cooled slightly on the baking sheet, move them to a wire rack to finish cooling.

Einkorn Peanut Butter Cookies:

Ingredients:

- 1 1/2 cups einkorn flour
- 1/2 tsp baking soda
- 1/2 tsp salt
- 1/2 cup unsalted butter, softened
- 1/2 cup granulated sugar
- 1/2 cup packed brown sugar
- 1/2 cup peanut butter
- One large egg
- 1 tsp vanilla extract

Instructions:

1. Set the oven's temperature to 350°F (175°C). Use parchment paper to cover a baking sheet.
2. Combine einkorn flour, baking soda, and salt in a bowl.
3. Combine the softened butter, granulated sugar, brown sugar, and peanut butter in a separate dish and beat until fluffy.
4. Continue beating after adding the egg and vanilla essence.
5. Gradually incorporate the dry mixture into the wet one.
6. Form the dough into 1-inch balls and set them on the baking sheet that has been prepared.
7. Use a fork to flatten each ball and make a crisscross pattern.
8. Bake for 10 to 12 minutes, until the sides are just beginning to turn golden.

9. After the cookies have cooled slightly on the baking sheet, move them to a wire rack to finish cooling.

Einkorn Snickerdoodles:

Ingredients:
- 1 1/2 cups einkorn flour
- 1/2 tsp baking soda
- 1/4 tsp cream of tartar
- 1/2 cup unsalted butter, softened
- 3/4 cup granulated sugar
- One large egg
- 1 tsp vanilla extract
- For coating: 2 tbsp granulated sugar + 1 tsp ground cinnamon

Instructions:
1. Set the oven's temperature to 350°F (175°C). Use parchment paper to cover a baking sheet.
2. Combine einkorn flour, baking soda, and cream of tartar in a bowl.
3. Combine the softened butter, granulated sugar, and vanilla extract in a separate dish and beat until well combined and fluffy.
4. Add the egg and mix thoroughly.
5. Gradually incorporate the dry mixture into the wet one.
6. To prepare the coating, combine the two tablespoons of ground cinnamon and granulated sugar in a small basin.
7. Roll the dough into balls 1 inch in diameter in the cinnamon-sugar mixture.
8. Set the coated balls on the lined baking sheet and gently press them down.
9. Bake for 10 to 12 minutes or until the sides are slightly browned and firm.

10. After the cookies have cooled slightly on the baking sheet, move them to a wire rack to finish cooling.

Einkorn Chocolate Brownies:

Ingredients:
- 1 cup einkorn flour
- 1/2 cup unsweetened cocoa powder
- 1/2 tsp salt
- 1/2 cup unsalted butter
- 1 cup granulated sugar
- Two large eggs
- 1 tsp vanilla extract
- 1/2 cup chopped nuts (optional)

Instructions:
1. Set the oven's temperature to 350°F (175°C)—butter and flour in an 8-inch baking dish.
2. Combine einkorn flour, cocoa powder, and salt in a basin.
3. Melt the butter in a saucepan over low heat. Granulated sugar is added when the heat is turned off and mixed well.
4. Stir in the vanilla essence after adding each egg one at a time.
5. Stir to blend after adding the dry ingredients in small amounts to the wet mixture. Fold in the chopped nuts, if desired.
6. Spoon the batter equally into the baking dish that has been prepared.
7. Bake for 25 to 30 minutes or until moist crumbs come from a toothpick inserted in the center.
8. After the brownies have finished cooling in the pan, cut them into squares.

Einkorn Apple Crisp:

Ingredients:

- 4 cups sliced apples (peeled and cored)
- 1 tsp lemon juice
- 1/2 cup einkorn flour
- 1/2 cup rolled oats
- 1/2 cup granulated sugar
- 1/4 cup unsalted butter, softened
- 1/2 tsp ground cinnamon
- 1/4 tsp ground nutmeg
- Vanilla ice cream (optional for serving)

Instructions:

1. Set the oven's temperature to 350°F (175°C).
2. Place the apple slices in a greased 8-inch baking dish after tossing them with lemon juice.
3. Combine einkorn flour, rolled oats, sugar, butter that has been softened, cinnamon, and nutmeg in a bowl. Mix the ingredients until they resemble coarse crumbs.
4. Evenly distribute the crumb mixture over the apples.
5. Bake for 35 to 40 minutes until the apples are soft and the topping is golden.
6. If desired, top with a dollop of vanilla ice cream while still warm.

Einkorn Peach Cobbler:

Ingredients:

- 4 cups sliced peeled peaches
- 1/2 cup granulated sugar
- 1/2 cup einkorn flour
- 1/2 tsp baking powder
- 1/4 tsp salt
- 1/2 cup milk

- 1/4 cup unsalted butter, melted

Instructions:

1. Set the oven's temperature to 350°F (175°C).
2. Place sliced peaches and 1/4 cup of granulated sugar in a bowl. Place aside.
3. Combine the remaining 1/4 cup of granulated sugar, baking powder, and salt in a separate dish with the einkorn flour.
4. Once the batter is smooth, add the milk and melted butter.
5. Spoon the batter into an 8x8-inch baking dish that has been buttered.
6. Spread the batter with the peach mixture.
7. Bake for 40 to 45 minutes or until the peaches are bubbling and the topping is golden brown.
8. Before serving, let the cobbler cool somewhat.

Einkorn Cherry Pie:

Ingredients:

- 2 1/2 cups einkorn flour
- 1 tsp salt
- 1 cup unsalted butter, cold and cubed
- 6-7 tbsp ice water
- 4 cups fresh or frozen pitted cherries
- 1 cup granulated sugar
- 1/4 cup cornstarch
- 1/4 tsp almond extract
- 1/2 tsp vanilla extract
- 1 tbsp butter

Instructions:

1. Combine salt and einkorn flour in a big bowl. Until the mixture resembles coarse crumbs, gradually include the cold butter.
2. Continue mixing as you gradually add ice water until the dough comes together. The dough should be divided in half, wrapped in plastic, and chilled for at least an hour.
3. Set the oven's temperature to 425°F (220°C).
4. To fit a 9-inch pie dish, roll out one dough ball on a floured board. Set it inside the dish.
5. Combine cherries, cornstarch, sugar, almond extract, and vanilla extract in a bowl. Fill the pie crust with the ingredients.
6. Add butter dots to the filling.
7. After rolling it out, spread the second dough ball on top of the filling. To seal the pie, trim and crimp the edges.
8. To let steam out, make a few slits in the top Crust.
9. Bake for 45 to 55 minutes or until the filling is bubbling and the Crust is golden brown.
10. Let the pie cool completely before slicing.

Einkorn Pumpkin Pie:

Ingredients:

- 1 1/2 cups einkorn flour
- 1/2 tsp salt
- 1/2 cup unsalted butter, cold and cubed
- 3 tbsp ice water
- 2 cups canned pumpkin puree
- 1 cup granulated sugar
- 1 tsp ground cinnamon
- 1/2 tsp ground ginger
- 1/4 tsp ground cloves

- 1/4 tsp salt
- Two large eggs
- 1 cup evaporated milk

Instructions:

1. Combine salt and einkorn flour in a big bowl. Until the mixture resembles coarse crumbs, gradually include the cold butter.
2. Continue mixing as you gradually add ice water until the dough comes together. The dough should be shaped into a disc, covered in plastic wrap, and chilled for at least 30 minutes.
3. Set the oven's temperature to 425°F (220°C).
4. To fit a 9-inch pie dish, roll out the dough on a surface dusted with flour. Set it inside the dish.
5. Combine pumpkin puree, granulated sugar, cinnamon, ginger, cloves, and salt in another bowl.
6. Add the eggs and blend thoroughly before adding the evaporated milk.
7. Fill the pie crust with the pumpkin mixture.
8. Bake for 15 minutes at 425 °F (220 °C), then lower the heat to 350 °F (175 °C) and continue baking for an additional 40 to 50 minutes, or until a knife inserted close to the middle comes out clean.
9. Let the pie cool completely before slicing.

Einkorn Pecan Pie:

Ingredients:

- 1 1/2 cups einkorn flour
- 1/2 tsp salt
- 1/2 cup unsalted butter, cold and cubed
- 3 tbsp ice water
- 1 cup granulated sugar

- 1 cup corn syrup
- 1/2 tsp salt
- Three large eggs
- 1 tsp vanilla extract
- 1 1/2 cups pecan halves

Instructions:

1. Combine salt and einkorn flour in a big bowl. Until the mixture resembles coarse crumbs, gradually include the cold butter.
2. Continue mixing as you gradually add ice water until the dough comes together. The dough should be shaped into a disc, covered in plastic wrap, and chilled for at least 30 minutes.
3. Set the oven's temperature to 350°F (175°C).
4. To fit a 9-inch pie dish, roll out the dough on a surface dusted with flour. Set it inside the dish.
5. Combine the granulated sugar, corn syrup, salt, eggs, and vanilla essence in a bowl by whisking everything together thoroughly.
6. Evenly distribute pecan halves over the pie crust.
7. Sprinkle the pecans with the sugar mixture.
8. Bake the filling for 50 to 60 minutes or until it is firm and puffy.
9. Let the pie cool completely before slicing.

Einkorn Key Lime Pie:

Ingredients:

- 1 1/2 cups einkorn flour
- 1/2 tsp salt
- 1/2 cup unsalted butter, cold and cubed
- 3 tbsp ice water
- Four large egg yolks

- One can (14 ounces) sweetened condensed milk
- 1/2 cup fresh key lime juice
- Zest of 2 key limes
- Whipped cream for topping (optional)

Instructions:

1. Combine salt and einkorn flour in a big bowl. Until the mixture resembles coarse crumbs, gradually include the cold butter.
2. Continue mixing as you gradually add ice water until the dough comes together. The dough should be shaped into a disc, covered in plastic wrap, and chilled for at least 30 minutes.
3. Set the oven's temperature to 350°F (175°C).
4. To fit a 9-inch pie dish, roll out the dough on a surface dusted with flour. Crimp the edges and put it in the dish.
5. Combine the egg yolks, sweetened condensed milk, key lime juice, and key lime zest in a bowl by thoroughly whisking the ingredients.
6. Fill the pie shell with the filling.
7. Bake the filling for 15 to 20 minutes or until it is set.
8. After letting the pie cool, put it in the fridge for at least two hours before serving. If desired, garnish with whipped cream.

Einkorn Cheesecake:
Ingredients:

For the Crust:

- 1 1/2 cups Einkorn cookie crumbs (you can use Einkorn graham crackers or any Einkorn cookies)
- 1/4 cup unsalted butter, melted

- 1/4 cup granulated sugar

Ingredients:

For the Filling:

- 4 (8-ounce) packages of cream cheese, softened
- 1 1/4 cups granulated sugar
- 1 tsp vanilla extract
- Four large eggs

Instructions:

For the Crust:

1. To start, preheat the oven to 350°F (175°C). Prepare a greased 9-inch springform pan.
2. Combine the melted butter, sugar, and einkorn cookie crumbs in a bowl. Press the mixture firmly into the bottom of the prepared pan.
3. After baking for 10 minutes, remove the dish and set it aside to cool while you prepare the filling.

Instructions:

For the Filling:

1. Lower the oven's setting to 325°F (160°C).
2. In a sizable mixing basin, smooth up the softened cream cheese.
3. Continue beating after adding the vanilla extract and granulated sugar.
4. Beat well after each addition of the eggs, one at a time.

5. Cover the baked Crust with the cream cheese mixture.
6. Bake for 45 to 50 minutes until the center is slightly shaky, and the sides are set.
7. After an extra hour, turn off the oven and leave the cheesecake inside.
8. Take it out of the oven, allowing it to cool completely at room temperature, and then chill it for several hours or overnight.

Einkorn Tiramisu:

Ingredients:

- 1 1/2 cups strong brewed coffee, cooled
- 1/4 cup coffee liqueur (optional)
- Three large egg yolks
- 1/2 cup granulated sugar
- 1 cup mascarpone cheese
- 1 cup heavy cream
- 1 tsp vanilla extract
- 24-30 einkorn ladyfinger cookies
- Unsweetened cocoa powder for dusting
- Dark chocolate shavings for garnish (optional)

Instructions:

1. Combine the brewed coffee and coffee liqueur (if using) in a small bowl.
2. Combine egg yolks and granulated sugar in a heatproof basin.
3. Set up a double boiler by placing the bowl over a pot of hot water. Whisk continually until the mixture turns pale and slightly thickens. Take it off the stove and let it cool.
4. Smooth out the mascarpone cheese in a different bowl.
5. Whip heavy cream and vanilla extract to stiff peaks in another bowl.

6. Gently stir the whipped cream into the mascarpone cheese until thoroughly incorporated.
7. Place a layer of ladyfingers on the bottom of a serving dish after gently dipping each one in the coffee mixture.
8. Cover the ladyfingers with half of the mascarpone mixture.
9. Repeat step 9 with an additional layer of ladyfingers dipped in mascarpone.
10. Protect with a lid and keep chilled for at least 4 hours or overnight.
11. Before serving, sprinkle unsweetened cocoa powder on top and, if you like, decorate with dark chocolate shavings.

Einkorn Cannoli:
Ingredients:

for the Cannoli Shells:

- 2 cups Einkorn flour
- 2 tbsp granulated sugar
- 1/4 tsp salt
- 2 tbsp unsalted butter, softened
- 1/2 cup white wine
- Vegetable oil for frying

Ingredients:

for the Cannoli Filling:

- 2 cups ricotta cheese
- 1/2 cup powdered sugar
- 1/2 tsp vanilla extract

- 1/4 cup mini chocolate chips (optional)
- Powdered sugar for dusting

Instructions:

For the Cannoli Shells:

1. Combine einkorn flour, salt, and granulated sugar in a bowl.
2. Stir the mixture until it resembles coarse crumbs before adding the softened butter.
3. Stirring constantly, and gradually add white wine until dough forms. All of the wine might be optional.
4. Slightly knead the dough on a floured surface until it is smooth. Please put it in the fridge for 30 minutes after wrapping it in plastic.
5. On a floured surface, very thinly roll out the dough. Use a glass or a cookie cutter to make circles.
6. Apply a little water to the edges of each circle before wrapping it over a cannoli mold.
7. Bring vegetable oil to 350°F (175°C) in a deep fryer or a heavy pot.
8. Gently cook the cannoli shells in hot oil until they are golden brown. Use a slotted spoon to remove and drain on paper towels.
9. After the shells have cooled, carefully remove them from the molds.

Instructions:

For the Cannoli Filling:

1. Ricotta cheese, powdered sugar, and vanilla essence should be thoroughly combined in a bowl.

2. Add micro chocolate chips if desired.
3. Add the ricotta mixture to the cooled cannoli shells using a piping bag.
4. Before serving, sprinkle powdered sugar over the filled cannoli.

Einkorn Gelato:

Ingredients:

- 2 cups Einkorn flour
- 2 cups whole milk
- 1 cup heavy cream
- 3/4 cup granulated sugar
- One vanilla bean, split and scraped
- Pinch of salt

Instructions:

1. In a mixing bowl, thoroughly combine the Einkorn flour and sugar.
2. Bring the milk, heavy cream, vanilla bean (seeds and pod), and salt to a simmer in a saucepan over medium heat.
3. While whisking continuously, slowly pour the hot milk mixture over the Einkorn mixture.
4. Return the mixture to the pan and simmer it over low heat, stirring frequently, until it takes on the consistency of custard.
5. Take the mixture off the heat, strain it to get the vanilla bean pod out, and let it cool.
6. After the mixture has cooled, churn it in an ice cream maker, following the directions provided by the device.
7. Place the churned gelato in a container with a lid and freeze until solid.

Einkorn Affogato:

Ingredients:

- 1 scoop Einkorn gelato
- 1 shot of hot espresso

Instructions:

1. Fill a serving cup or tumbler with a scoop of Einkorn gelato.
2. Sprinkle the gelato with a hot espresso shot.
3. Serve your Einkorn Affogato right away and enjoy!

Einkorn Lemon Sorbet:

Ingredients:

- 2 cups Einkorn flour
- 2 cups water
- 1 1/2 cups granulated sugar
- Zest and juice of 4 lemons

Instructions:

1. Combine Einkorn flour, water, and sugar in a saucepan. Stirring constantly, cook over medium heat until the sugar dissolves.
2. Add the lemon juice and zest after removing from the heat. Stir thoroughly.
3. After allowing the mixture to reach room temperature, put it in the fridge for at least two hours.
4. Use an ice cream machine to churn the mixture, following the manufacturer's instructions.
5. Place the sorbet in a jar with a lid and freeze until solid.

Einkorn Strawberry Sorbet:

Ingredients:

- 2 cups Einkorn flour
- 2 cups water
- 1 1/2 cups granulated sugar
- 2 cups fresh strawberries, hulled and pureed

Instructions:

1. Combine Einkorn flour, water, and sugar in a saucepan. Stirring constantly, cook over medium heat until the sugar dissolves.
2. Remove from the heat and stir in the pureed fresh strawberries. Stir thoroughly.
3. After allowing the mixture to reach room temperature, put it in the fridge for at least two hours.
4. Use an ice cream machine to churn the mixture according to the manufacturer's instructions.
5. Spoon the strawberry sorbet into a container with a lid and freeze until solid.

Einkorn Chocolate Gelato:

Ingredients:

- 2 cups Einkorn flour
- 2 cups whole milk
- 1 cup heavy cream
- 3/4 cup granulated sugar
- 1/2 cup unsweetened cocoa powder
- Pinch of salt

Instructions:
1. Thoroughly combine Einkorn flour, sugar, and cocoa powder in a mixing basin.
2. Heat the milk, heavy cream, and salt in a saucepan over medium heat until it steams.
3. While whisking continuously, slowly pour the hot milk mixture over the Einkorn mixture.
4. Return the mixture to the pan and simmer it over low heat, stirring frequently, until it takes on the consistency of custard.
5. Please turn off the heat and let it cool.
6. After the mixture has cooled, churn it in an ice cream maker per the directions provided by the device.
7. Place the chocolate gelato in a container with a lid and freeze until solid.

Einkorn Coffee Ice Cream:

Ingredients:
- 2 cups Einkorn flour
- 2 cups whole milk
- 1 cup heavy cream
- 3/4 cup granulated sugar
- Two tablespoons of instant coffee granules
- Pinch of salt

Instructions:
1. Thoroughly combine sugar, instant coffee granules, and Einkorn flour in a mixing dish.
2. Heat the milk, heavy cream, and salt in a saucepan over medium heat until it steams.
3. While whisking continuously, slowly pour the hot milk mixture over the Einkorn mixture.

4. Return the mixture to the pan and simmer it over low heat, stirring frequently, until it takes on the consistency of custard.
5. Turn off the heat and let it cool.
6. After the mixture has cooled, churn it in an ice cream maker under the directions provided by the device.
7. Place the coffee ice cream in a container with a lid and freeze until solid.

Einkorn Mint Chocolate Chip Ice Cream:

Ingredients:
- 2 cups Einkorn flour
- 2 cups whole milk
- 1 cup heavy cream
- 3/4 cup granulated sugar
- One teaspoon of peppermint extract
- Green food coloring (optional)
- 1/2 cup chocolate chips

Instructions:
1. In a mixing bowl, thoroughly combine the Einkorn flour and sugar.
2. Bring the milk, heavy cream, and peppermint extract to a simmer in a saucepan over medium heat.
3. While whisking continuously, slowly pour the hot milk mixture over the Einkorn mixture.
4. Add green food coloring for the hue of mint, if desired.
5. Return the mixture to the pan and cook it over low heat, stirring frequently, until it takes on the consistency of custard.
6. Turn off the heat and let it cool.
7. After the mixture has cooled, churn it in an ice cream maker following the manufacturer's directions, adding the chocolate chips in the final few minutes.

8. Spoon the mint chocolate chip ice cream into a container with a cover and freeze until solid.

Einkorn Pistachio Ice Cream:

Ingredients:
- 2 cups Einkorn flour
- 2 cups whole milk
- 1 cup heavy cream
- 3/4 cup granulated sugar
- 1 cup shelled pistachios, finely chopped
- One teaspoon of almond extract
- Green food coloring (optional)

Instructions:
1. In a mixing bowl, thoroughly combine the Einkorn flour and sugar.
2. Bring the milk, heavy cream, and almond extract to a simmer in a saucepan over medium heat.
3. While whisking continuously, slowly pour the hot milk mixture over the Einkorn mixture.
4. To achieve the pistachio hue, if desired, add green food coloring.
5. Return the mixture to the pan and cook it over low heat, stirring frequently, until it takes on the consistency of custard.
6. Turn off the heat and let it cool.
7. After the mixture has cooled, churn it in an ice cream maker per the manufacturer's directions while incorporating the chopped pistachios in the final few minutes.
8. Spoon the pistachio ice cream into a covered container and freeze for several hours to solidify.

Einkorn Banana Split:

Ingredients:

- Two ripe bananas, split in half lengthwise
- Four scoops of Einkorn vanilla ice cream
- Chocolate sauce
- Strawberry sauce
- Crushed pineapple
- Whipped cream
- Maraschino cherries
- Chopped nuts (optional)

Instructions:

1. Arrange the banana halves on a banana split boat or in a serving dish.
2. Top each banana half with a spoonful of Einkorn vanilla ice cream.
3. Drizzle with strawberry and chocolate sauce.
4. Include pineapple chunks.
5. Garnish with whipped cream, maraschino cherries, and chopped nuts if preferred.
6. Serve your Einkorn Banana Split right away and savor it!

Einkorn Root Beer Float:

Ingredients:

- Two scoops of Einkorn vanilla ice cream
- One can or bottle of root beer

Instructions:

1. Fill a tall glass or mug with two Einkorn vanilla ice cream scoops.
2. Pour the root beer on top of the ice cream gradually.

3. After settling the foam, serve it immediately with a straw and a long spoon.

Einkorn Chocolate Milkshake:

Ingredients:
- 2 cups Einkorn chocolate ice cream
- 1 cup whole milk
- Two tablespoons of chocolate syrup
- Whipped cream (optional)
- Chocolate shavings (optional)

Instructions:
1. Blend whole milk, chocolate syrup, and Einkorn chocolate ice cream in a blender.
2. Blend until creamy and smooth.
3. Pour into a glass, then, if you like, top with whipped cream and chocolate shavings.
4. Immediately serve with a straw.

Einkorn Vanilla Smoothie:

Ingredients:
- 1 cup Einkorn vanilla ice cream
- 1/2 cup milk
- One ripe banana
- 1/2 teaspoon vanilla extract
- Honey or maple syrup (optional for sweetness)

Instructions:
1. Blend milk, ripe banana, vanilla extract, and Einkorn vanilla ice cream in a blender.

2. If more sweetness is wanted, add honey or maple syrup.
3. Blend till fluid.
4. Transfer to a glass and serve right away.

Einkorn Berry Blast Smoothie:

Ingredients:
- 1 cup Einkorn vanilla ice cream
- 1/2 cup milk
- 1/2 cup mixed berries (strawberries, blueberries, raspberries)
- 1/2 banana
- One tablespoon honey (optional for sweetness)

Instructions:
1. Blend Einkorn vanilla ice cream, milk, mixed berries, banana, and optional honey until smooth.
2. Blend the ingredients until well combined and smooth.
3. Transfer to a glass and serve right away.

Einkorn Green Smoothie:

Ingredients:
- 1 cup Einkorn vanilla ice cream
- 1/2 cup milk
- 1 cup fresh spinach leaves
- 1/2 banana
- 1/2 cup pineapple chunks
- One tablespoon honey (optional for sweetness)

Instructions:

1. Blend Einkorn vanilla ice cream, milk, banana, pineapple chunks, and optional honey with fresh spinach leaves.
2. Blend the smoothie until it's smooth and green.
3. Transfer to a glass and serve right away.

Einkorn Mango Lassi:

Ingredients:

- 1 cup Einkorn vanilla ice cream
- One ripe mango, peeled and diced
- 1/2 cup plain yogurt
- 1/2 cup milk
- Two tablespoons honey (adjust to taste)
- 1/4 teaspoon ground cardamom (optional)

Instructions:

1. Combine milk, honey, Einkorn vanilla ice cream, diced mango, plain yogurt, and, if desired, ground cardamom.
2. Purée the mixture until it's smooth and creamy.
3. After tasting, adjust the sweetness by adding more honey, if necessary.
4. Fill glasses with chilled Einkorn Mango Lassi and serve.

Einkorn Kiwi Cooler:

Ingredients:

- Two ripe kiwis, peeled and diced
- 1 cup Einkorn vanilla ice cream
- 1/2 cup pineapple juice
- 1/2 cup sparkling water or club soda
- One tablespoon honey (adjust to taste)
- Ice cubes

Instructions:

1. Blend diced kiwis, Einkorn vanilla ice cream, pineapple juice, honey, and ice cubes until smooth.
2. Purée until fluid.
3. Fill the glasses with the mixture, leaving room at the top.
4. Top each glass with sparkling water or club soda to add a fizzy kick.
5. Gently stir, then serve right away.

Einkorn Watermelon Slushie:

Ingredients:

- 2 cups seedless watermelon chunks
- 1 cup Einkorn vanilla ice cream
- 1/2 cup water
- Two tablespoons of lime juice
- 1-2 tablespoons honey (adjust to taste)
- Ice cubes

Instructions:

1. Blend watermelon pieces, Einkorn vanilla ice cream, ice cubes, lime juice, honey, and water in a blender.
2. Purée the mixture until it has the consistency of a slushie.
3. Taste, and if necessary, add additional honey to balance sweetness.
4. Pour your Einkorn Watermelon Slush into glasses and serve right away.

Einkorn Blueberry Lemonade:

Ingredients:

- 1 cup Einkorn vanilla ice cream
- 1/2 cup blueberries (fresh or frozen)

- 1/2 cup lemonade
- One tablespoon of lemon zest
- 1-2 tablespoons honey (adjust to taste)
- Ice cubes

Instructions:

1. Blend Einkorn vanilla ice cream, blueberries, lemonade, honey, and ice cubes in a blender.
2. Purée until fluid.
3. Taste, and if necessary, add additional honey to balance sweetness.
4. Pour cold Einkorn Blueberry Lemonade into glasses and serve.

Einkorn Raspberry Iced Tea:

Ingredients:

- 1 cup Einkorn vanilla ice cream
- 1/2 cup fresh raspberries
- 1 cup brewed and chilled black tea
- 1-2 tablespoons honey (adjust to taste)
- Ice cubes

Instructions:

1. Blend Einkorn vanilla ice cream, fresh raspberries, iced black tea, honey, and a pinch of salt in a blender.
2. Purée until fluid.
3. Taste, and if necessary, add additional honey to balance sweetness.
4. Pour cooled Einkorn Raspberry Iced Tea into glasses and serve.

Einkorn Peach Punch:

Ingredients:

- 1 cup Einkorn vanilla ice cream
- One ripe peach, peeled and diced
- 1/2 cup orange juice
- 1/4 cup pineapple juice
- 1-2 tablespoons honey (adjust to taste)
- Ice cubes

Instructions:

1. Blend ice cubes, honey, orange juice, pineapple juice, Einkorn vanilla ice cream, and chopped peaches in a blender.
2. Purée until fluid.
3. Taste, and if necessary, add additional honey to balance sweetness.
4. Pour cold Einkorn Peach Punch into glasses and serve.

Einkorn Cucumber Mint Cooler:

Ingredients:

- 1 cup Einkorn vanilla ice cream
- 1/2 cucumber, peeled and diced
- 1/4 cup fresh mint leaves
- 1/4 cup water
- 1-2 tablespoons honey (adjust to taste)
- Ice cubes

Instructions:

1. Blend sliced cucumber, mint, Einkorn vanilla ice cream, water, honey, and ice cubes in a blender.
2. Purée until fluid.
3. Taste, and if necessary, add additional honey to balance sweetness.

4. Pour chilled Einkorn Cucumber Mint Cooler into glasses and serve.

Einkorn Pineapple Paradise:

Ingredients:

- 1 cup Einkorn vanilla ice cream
- 1 cup pineapple chunks (fresh or frozen)
- 1/2 cup coconut milk
- 1-2 tablespoons honey (adjust to taste)
- Ice cubes

Instructions:

1. Blend Einkorn vanilla ice cream, pineapple pieces, coconut milk, honey, and ice cubes until smooth.
2. Purée until fluid.
3. Taste, and if necessary, add additional honey to balance sweetness.
4. Pour cold Einkorn Pineapple Paradise into glasses and serve.

Einkorn Cranberry Spritzer:

Ingredients:

- 1 cup Einkorn vanilla ice cream
- 1/2 cup cranberry juice
- 1/2 cup sparkling water or club soda
- 1-2 tablespoons honey (adjust to taste)
- Ice cubes

Instructions:

1. Blend Einkorn vanilla ice cream, cranberry juice, honey, and ice cubes in a blender.

2. Purée until fluid.
3. Fill the glasses with the mixture, leaving room at the top.
4. Top each glass with sparkling water or club soda to add a fizzy kick.
5. Give your Einkorn Cranberry Spritzer a gentle stir before serving.

Einkorn Hot Chocolate:

Ingredients:

- 2 cups of milk (any milk of your choice)
- Two tablespoons of Einkorn flour
- Two tablespoons of unsweetened cocoa powder
- Two tablespoons sugar (adjust to taste)
- 1/4 teaspoon vanilla extract
- A pinch of salt
- Whipped cream and chocolate shavings for garnish (optional)

Instructions:

1. Combine Einkorn flour, cocoa powder, sugar, and a dash of salt in a saucepan.
2. Pour the milk in gradually while whisking constantly to prevent lumps.
3. Heat the mixture to a moderate simmer in the saucepan over medium heat. Until it thickens and smoothes, stir regularly.
4. Take the mixture off the heat, add the vanilla essence, and then pour it into cups.
5. If preferred, garnish with whipped cream and chocolate shavings. Serve warm.

Einkorn Chai Latte:

Ingredients:

- 1 cup of milk (any milk of your choice)
- One chai tea bag or one tablespoon of loose chai tea
- Two teaspoons of Einkorn flour
- 1-2 tablespoons honey or sugar (adjust to taste)
- A pinch of ground cinnamon (optional)

Instructions:

1. Heat the milk in a small saucepan until it is ready to boil. Get rid of the heat.
2. Pour the heated milk over the chai tea bag or loose tea and let it simmer for 5-7 minutes.
3. Take out the teabag or pour the loose tea leaves into a strainer.
4. To make a paste, combine some cold milk with the Einkorn flour in a separate basin.
5. Return the milk to low heat after whisking the Einkorn paste and chai.
6. Add honey or sugar and whisk regularly while heating the mixture until it slightly thickens.
7. Pour into a mug, top with some freshly ground cinnamon, and serve hot.

Einkorn Cappuccino:

Ingredients:

- One shot of espresso or 1/2 cup of strong-brewed coffee
- 1/2 cup milk (any milk of your choice)
- 1-2 teaspoons Einkorn flour
- Sugar or sweetener to taste

Instructions:

1. Make a strong cup of coffee or an espresso shot.
2. Warm the milk in a small pot until it is warm but not boiling.
3. To make a paste, combine some cold milk with the Einkorn flour in a separate basin.
4. Stir the Einkorn paste into the hot milk, then keep heating and stirring the mixture until it slightly thickens.
5. Add the Einkorn milk mixture to the espresso or coffee in the cup.
6. Stir in sugar or another sweetener to taste.

Einkorn Mocha:

Ingredients:

- One shot of espresso or 1/2 cup of strong-brewed coffee

- 1/2 cup milk (any milk of your choice)
- Two tablespoons of unsweetened cocoa powder
- 1-2 teaspoons Einkorn flour
- Sugar or sweetener to taste
- Whipped cream and chocolate shavings for garnish (optional)

Instructions:

1. Make a strong cup of coffee or an espresso shot.
2. Combine Einkorn wheat and chocolate powder in a small pot.
3. Add the milk gradually while stirring to prevent lumps.
4. Heat the mixture to a moderate simmer in the saucepan over medium heat. Up till it thickens, stir frequently.
5. Take the espresso or coffee off the fire and pour it into a cup.
6. Place the Einkorn cocoa milk mixture on top and, to taste, add sugar or another sweetener.
7. If preferred, garnish with whipped cream and chocolate shavings.

Einkorn Matcha Latte:

Ingredients:

- One teaspoon of matcha green tea powder
- 1 cup milk (any milk of your choice)
- 1-2 teaspoons Einkorn flour
- Honey or sweetener to taste (optional)

Instructions:

1. To make a paste, combine a little cold milk and Einkorn flour in a bowl.

2. Heat the remaining milk in another pan until it is warm but not boiling.
3. Put some hot water and matcha powder in a cup. Matcha should be thoroughly mixed and completely lump-free.
4. Stir the hot milk with the Einkorn paste until it slightly thickens.
5. Add the Einkorn milk mixture on top of the matcha in the cup.

Einkorn Herbal Tea:

Ingredients:

- 1-2 teaspoons Einkorn flour (as a thickener)
- Your favorite herbal tea bag or loose herbal tea leaves
- Water (amount as per tea package instructions)
- Honey or sweetener to taste (optional)

Instructions:
1. Prepare your preferred herbal tea as directed on the packaging.
2. To make a paste, combine a tiny amount of cold water with the Einkorn flour in a small bowl.
3. Take out the tea bag or filter the loose tea leaves once the tea has steeped.
4. Add the Einkorn paste to the brewed tea and reheat it over low heat.
5. Continue stirring until the tea starts to slightly thicken.
6. Remove from the heat and, if preferred, add honey or another sweetness.
7. Provide hot Einkorn herbal tea.

Einkorn Lavender Infusion:

Ingredients:

- 1-2 teaspoons dried culinary lavender buds
- 1 cup hot water
- Honey or sweetener to taste (optional)

Instructions:
1. Put the dried lavender buds in a heat-resistant container or a tea infuser.
2. Cover the lavender with boiling water, then steep it for 5 to 7 minutes.
3. Take out the lavender and, if preferred, add honey or another sweetener.
4. Take pleasure in your calming Einkorn Lavender Infusion.

Einkorn Lemon Ginger Elixir:

Ingredients:

- 1-2 teaspoons Einkorn flour
- 1 cup hot water
- One slice of fresh ginger
- One slice of lemon
- Honey or sweetener to taste (optional)

Instructions:
1. Mix cold water and Einkorn flour in a cup to make a paste.

2. Heat the water to a warm but not boiling temperature.
3. Add the ginger and lemon slices to the hot water and let them steep for a few minutes.
4. Please remove the lemon and ginger, then whisk in the Einkorn paste until it thickens slightly.
5. If preferred, add honey or another sweetness.
6. Drink some Einkorn Lemon Ginger Elixir to relax.

Einkorn Detox Smoothie:

Ingredients:

- One banana
- 1 cup spinach leaves
- 1/2 cup pineapple chunks (fresh or frozen)
- 1/2 cup almond milk (or any milk of your choice)
- 1-2 teaspoons Einkorn flour
- 1/2 teaspoon honey (optional for added sweetness)
-

Instructions:
1. Fill a blender with all the ingredients.
2. Blend until creamy and smooth.
3. If additional sweetness is wanted, taste and add honey.
4. Pour your nutritious Einkorn Detox Smoothie into a glass and sip.

Einkorn Energy Booster:

Ingredients:

- 1-2 teaspoons Einkorn flour
- 1 cup brewed green tea (chilled)
- One tablespoon honey
- Juice of 1/2 lemon
- Ice cubes

Instructions:

1. Mix cold water and Einkorn flour in a glass to make a paste.
2. Fill the glass with the iced green tea, honey, and lemon juice.
3. Stir to fully incorporate the Einkorn paste.
4. Fill the glass with ice cubes and swirl to cold.
5. Drink some Einkorn Energy Booster to revive yourself.

Einkorn Immune-Boosting Elixir:

Ingredients:

- 1-2 teaspoons Einkorn flour
- 1 cup warm water
- Juice of 1/2 lemon
- One teaspoon of honey (optional)
- 1/2 teaspoon grated fresh turmeric (or 1/4 teaspoon ground turmeric)

1. To make a paste, combine warm water and Einkorn flour in a cup.
2. Fill the cup with lemon juice, honey, and freshly grated turmeric.
3. Stir to dissolve the Einkorn paste.
4. Take a warm drink of your immune-booster Einkorn elixir.

Einkorn Breakfast Burrito:

Ingredients:

- One large tortilla
- Two eggs scrambled
- 1/4 cup cooked Einkorn wheat berries
- 1/4 cup black beans, drained and rinsed
- 1/4 cup diced tomatoes
- 1/4 cup diced bell peppers
- 1/4 cup grated cheese (optional)
- Salt and pepper to taste
- Salsa or hot sauce for serving (optional)

Instructions:

1. The scrambled eggs, Einkorn wheat berries, black beans, chopped tomatoes, bell peppers, and grated cheese (if using) should be placed down the center of the tortilla, which should be laid flat.
2. Add salt and pepper to taste.
3. Fold the tortilla's sides and roll it up from the bottom

to make a burrito.

4. If preferred, cook the tortilla in a skillet or microwave for a warm, melty interior.
5. Put salsa or hot sauce on the side to serve.

Einkorn Breakfast Tacos:

Ingredients:

For the Scrambled Eggs:

- Four large eggs
- Salt and pepper to taste
- Two tablespoons milk
- One tablespoon butter
- 1/4 cup grated cheese (cheddar, Monterey Jack, or your choice)

For the Taco Filling:

- 1/2 cup cooked Einkorn wheat berries (prepared according to package instructions)
- 1/2 cup cooked and crumbled breakfast sausage
- 1/4 cup diced bell peppers
- 1/4 cup diced onions
- 1/4 cup diced tomatoes
- 1/4 cup chopped fresh cilantro (optional)
- Salsa for serving
- Four small flour or corn tortillas

Instructions:

1. Make the scrambled eggs first. Eggs, milk, salt, and pepper should all be thoroughly blended in a bowl.
2. Melt the butter in a nonstick skillet over low heat. Pour the egg mixture into the foaming, melted butter.
3. Use a spatula to gently whisk the eggs while they cook. Cook for 2 to 3 minutes or until barely set but still slightly creamy. After taking the pan off the heat, top the eggs with the cheese. To melt the cheese, place a lid on the skillet.
4. Warm the tortillas in a dry skillet over low heat or zap them in the microwave for 20 seconds to make them malleable while the eggs cook.
5. Cook the cooked Einkorn wheat berries, breakfast sausage, diced bell peppers, and onions in another skillet until the veggies are soft and the mixture is heated.
6. Spread some scrambled eggs and Einkorn and sausage mixture on each tortilla to create the tacos. If preferred, garnish with chopped tomatoes and fresh cilantro.
7. Place the salsa on the side and serve the breakfast tacos.

Einkorn Breakfast Quesadilla:

Ingredients:

For the Quesadilla Filling:

- Two large flour tortillas
- 1/2 cup cooked Einkorn wheat berries
- 1/2 cup cooked and crumbled bacon or breakfast sausage

- 1 cup shredded cheddar cheese
- 1/4 cup diced bell peppers
- 1/4 cup diced onions
- 1/4 cup diced tomatoes
- Salt and pepper to taste
- Cooking oil or butter for pan-frying

Instructions:

1. Heat a skillet with one tortilla over medium heat. Spread the tortilla with half of the cheese evenly.
2. Add diced bell peppers, onions, tomatoes, bacon or sausage, and Einkorn wheat berries. Add salt and pepper to taste.
3. Add the remaining cheese on top, then cover with the second tortilla.
4. Cook for about 2-3 minutes until the bottom tortilla is golden brown and the cheese is melting. The quesadilla should be carefully flipped over and cooked on the other side until golden brown and the cheese is melted.
5. Take the dish from the fire, allow it to cool briefly, and cut it into wedges. If preferred, serve with salsa or sour cream.

Einkorn Breakfast Hash:

Ingredients:

- 1 cup cooked Einkorn wheat berries
- 1 cup diced cooked potatoes
- 1/2 cup diced cooked ham or cooked breakfast sausage
- 1/4 cup diced onions
- 1/4 cup diced bell peppers
- Salt and pepper to taste
- Two tablespoons of cooking oil

- Optional: shredded cheese, hot sauce, or ketchup for serving

Instructions:

1. Heat the cooking oil in a skillet over medium heat. Saute the bell peppers and diced onions until they start to soften.
2. Add the diced potatoes, ham, sausage, and Einkorn wheat berries to the skillet. Add salt and pepper to taste.
3. Cook for 10 to 12 minutes, stirring regularly, or until everything is well cooked and has a lovely crispy texture.
4. Upon serving, garnish the breakfast hash with shredded cheese, spicy sauce, or ketchup as preferred.

Einkorn Breakfast Pizza:

Ingredients:

For the Pizza:

- One prepared pizza crust (store-bought or homemade)
- 1/2 cup tomato sauce
- 1 cup shredded mozzarella cheese
- 1/2 cup cooked Einkorn wheat berries
- 1/4 cup cooked breakfast sausage, crumbled
- Two large eggs
- Salt and pepper to taste
- Chopped fresh herbs (e.g., basil or parsley) for garnish

Instructions:

1. Set the oven to the recommended temperature for the pizza crust.
2. On a pizza stone or baking sheet, roll out the pizza crust. Over the Crust, evenly distribute the tomato sauce.
3. Top the sauce with half of the mozzarella cheese shavings. Then, scatter the breakfast sausage crumbles and cooked Einkorn wheat berries over the cheese.
4. Make two little wells in the toppings, one for each egg, and fill them with the toppings. Add salt and pepper to the eggs as desired.
5. Top the entire pizza with the leftover mozzarella cheese.
6. Bake the pie according to the directions on the pizza crust, usually 12 to 15 minutes, or until the Crust is brown and the eggs are done to your preference.
7. Take the dish out of the oven, slice it, and serve it.

Einkorn Breakfast Wrap:

Ingredients:

- One large whole wheat or Einkorn flour tortilla
- Two large eggs
- 1/4 cup cooked Einkorn wheat berries
- 1/4 cup diced cooked ham or cooked breakfast sausage
- 1/4 cup shredded cheddar cheese
- Salt and pepper to taste
- Optional: diced bell peppers, onions, or salsa for added flavor

Instructions:

1. In a bowl, combine eggs, cooked Einkorn wheat berries, diced ham or sausage, and any additional ingredients, such as bell peppers or onions. Add salt and pepper to taste.
2. Pour the egg mixture into a nonstick skillet already heated over medium-low heat.
3. Cook, carefully stirring, for two to three minutes or until the eggs are fully cooked and scrambled.
4. To make the tortilla more malleable, microwave it for 10 seconds or briefly heat it in a dry skillet.
5. Center the tortilla with the cooked egg mixture. On top, scatter the cheddar cheese shavings.
6. Fold the tortilla's sides and roll it up to make a breakfast wrap.
7. Immediately serve the breakfast wrap.

Einkorn Breakfast Casserole:

Ingredients:

- 2 cups cooked Einkorn wheat berries
- 1 cup cooked breakfast sausage, crumbled
- 1 cup shredded cheddar cheese
- 1/2 cup diced bell peppers
- 1/2 cup diced onions
- Six large eggs
- 1 cup milk
- Salt and pepper to taste

Instructions:

1. Grease a baking dish and preheat your oven to 350°F (175°C).
2. Put the cooked Einkorn wheat berries, crumbled breakfast sausage, shredded cheddar cheese, bell peppers, and diced onions in a sizable mixing dish.
3. Combine the eggs, milk, salt, and pepper in another bowl.
4. Top the Einkorn and sausage in the baking dish with the egg mixture.
5. Bake for 35 to 40 minutes, or until the casserole is set and the top is gently browned, in the preheated oven.
6. Before cutting and serving, allow it to cool for a few minutes.

Einkorn Breakfast Quiche:

Ingredients:

For the Quiche Filling:

- One prepared pie crust (store-bought or homemade)
- 1 cup cooked Einkorn wheat berries
- 1 cup cooked spinach, drained and chopped
- 1/2 cup diced ham or cooked breakfast sausage
- 1 cup shredded Swiss cheese

For the Quiche Custard:

- Four large eggs
- 1 cup milk
- Salt and pepper to taste
- 1/4 teaspoon ground nutmeg

Instructions:

1. Set the oven's temperature to 375°F (190°C).
2. Place pie weights or dried beans inside the prepared pie crust after lining it with parchment paper. After 10 minutes of blind baking, remove the parchment and weights from the Crust and bake it for 5 minutes.
3. Combine the cooked spinach, chopped ham or sausage, Einkorn wheat berries, and shredded Swiss cheese in a mixing bowl. The pre-baked pie shell should be covered with this mixture evenly.
4. Combine the eggs, milk, salt, pepper, and nutmeg separately.
5. Spoon the egg mixture on top of the pie filling.
6. Bake for 35 to 40 minutes, or until the quiche is set and the top is gently browned, in the preheated oven.
7. After cooling for a few minutes, slice and serve the quiche.

Einkorn Breakfast Strata:

Ingredients:

- 4 cups stale bread, cubed (Einkorn bread works great)
- 1 cup cooked Einkorn wheat berries
- 1 cup diced ham or cooked breakfast sausage
- 1 cup shredded cheddar cheese
- Six large eggs
- 2 cups milk
- One teaspoon of Dijon mustard
- Salt and pepper to taste
- 1/4 cup chopped fresh herbs (e.g., parsley or chives)

Instructions:

1. Arrange the stale bread cubes, cooked Einkorn wheat berries, diced ham or sausage, and shredded cheddar cheese in a greased baking dish.
2. Combine the eggs, milk, Dijon mustard, salt, and pepper in a bowl.
3. Pour the egg mixture over the ingredients arranged in the baking dish.
4. Place the baking dish in the refrigerator for at least 4 hours or overnight. Cover with plastic wrap.
5. Set the oven's temperature to 350°F (175°C).
6. In a preheated oven, take the strata out of the plastic wrap and bake it for 45 to 50 minutes, or until the top is golden brown and the center is set.
7. After a brief cooling period, garnish with fresh herbs and serve.

Einkorn Breakfast Sandwich:

Ingredients:

- Two whole wheat or Einkorn English muffins, split and toasted
- Two large eggs
- Two slices of cooked bacon or sausage patties
- Two slices of cheddar cheese
- Salt and pepper to taste
- Butter for toasting

1. Melt a little butter in a nonstick skillet over medium heat. Season the eggs with salt and pepper when cooked to the appropriate doneness. Crack the eggs into the skillet.
2. Place a slice of cheese on the bottom half of each toasted English muffin while the eggs cook.
3. Add a cooked egg, bacon or sausage patty, and cheese on top of the egg.
4. To make a sandwich, top with the remaining English muffin half.
5. Immediately serve the Einkorn breakfast sandwich.

Einkorn Breakfast Biscuits:

Ingredients:

For the Biscuits:

- 2 cups all-purpose Einkorn flour
- 2 1/2 teaspoons baking powder
- 1/2 teaspoon salt
- 1/2 cup unsalted butter, cold and cubed
- 3/4 cup milk

For the Breakfast Filling:

- Four large eggs scrambled
- Eight slices of cooked bacon or breakfast sausage patties
- 1 cup shredded cheddar cheese
- Salt and pepper to taste

Instructions:

1. Line a baking sheet with parchment paper and preheat your oven to 425°F (220°C).
2. Combine the Einkorn flour, baking soda, and salt in a mixing dish. Use a pastry cutter or fork to incorporate the cold, cubed butter into the dry ingredients until the mixture resembles coarse crumbs.
3. Add the milk and mix just until incorporated. Watch out for combining only a little.
4. Spread the biscuit dough on a floured surface and give it a couple of gentle kneads to bring it together. To a thickness of 1/2 inch, roll it out.
5. Rounds can be created with a biscuit cutter and placed on the baking pan after being cut out.
6. Bake the biscuits for 12 to 15 minutes or until golden brown.
7. Prepare the scrambled eggs, cook the bacon or sausage, and shred the cheese while the biscuits bake.
8. After baking the biscuits, cut them in half and allow them to cool somewhat. Add scrambled eggs, bacon, sausage, and grated cheese to each biscuit. Add salt and pepper to taste.
9. To make sandwiches, top the biscuits with the fillings and serve them hot.

Einkorn Breakfast Croissant:

Ingredients:

- Two large croissants
- Two large eggs
- Two slices of ham or bacon
- Two slices of cheddar or Swiss cheese
- Salt and pepper to taste

- Butter for toasting (optional)

Instructions:

1. Turn on the medium heat under a skillet. The croissants can be toasted in the skillet until lightly golden by brushing some butter on their cut sides.
2. Prepare the eggs in your preferred method (scrambled, fried, or poached) while the croissants are toasting. Add salt and pepper to taste.
3. Top the bottom half of each croissant with a slice of ham or bacon.
4. Add a fried egg and a slice of cheese on top.
5. To assemble a sandwich, top the ingredients with the croissant.
6. Warm up the Einkorn croissant for breakfast.

Einkorn Breakfast Bagel:

Ingredients:

- Two plain or whole grain Einkorn bagels, split and toasted
- Two large eggs
- Two slices of smoked salmon
- Two tablespoons of cream cheese
- Capers and thinly sliced red onion (optional)
- Salt and pepper to taste

Instructions:

1. Cover the bottom half of each toasted bagel with cream cheese.
2. Add a slice of smoked salmon on top.
3. Prepare the eggs as you choose (scrambled, fried, or poached), then top each bagel with one.

4. Taste for seasoning and, if preferred, add capers and thinly sliced red onion.
5. To assemble a sandwich, place the top half of the bagel on top of the fillings.
6. Immediately serve the Einkorn breakfast bagel.

Einkorn Breakfast Panini:

Ingredients:
- 2 ciabatta or Einkorn bread rolls
- Two large eggs
- Two slices of cooked bacon or ham

- Two slices of cheddar or provolone cheese
- Salt and pepper to taste
- Butter for grilling

Instructions:
1. Heat a grill pan or panini press.
2. While heating, prepare the eggs as you choose (scrambled, fried, or poached). Add salt and pepper to taste.
3. Cut the ciabatta, or Einkorn rolls in half, then layer a slice of cheese, a cooked egg, and a piece of bacon or ham on each half of the sandwich.
4. After placing the ingredients' top half of the rollover, cook the sandwiches in a grill pan or press them in a panini press until the cheese is melted and the bread is crisp.
5. Present the warm Einkorn breakfast panini.

Einkorn Breakfast Sausage|:

Ingredients:

- 1 pound ground Einkorn breakfast sausage
- Salt and pepper to taste
- Cooking oil (if needed)

Instructions:

1. Bring a skillet to a medium-high temperature.
2. You might need cooking oil to prevent sticking if your sausage is lean. Add the ground Einkorn breakfast sausage once the skillet is hot.
3. As the sausage cooks, use a spatula to break it into little crumbles. Add salt and pepper to taste.
4. Cook the sausage for 5-7 minutes or until it is well-heated and browned.
5. Take out of the skillet and pat any extra fat dry with paper towels. Use the cooked sausage as you see fit in your breakfast preparations.

Einkorn Breakfast Scramble:

Ingredients:

- Four large eggs
- 1/2 cup cooked Einkorn wheat berries
- 1/4 cup diced bell peppers
- 1/4 cup diced onions
- 1/4 cup diced tomatoes
- 1/4 cup shredded cheddar cheese
- Salt and pepper to taste
- Cooking oil or butter for the skillet

Instructions:

1. Combine the eggs, salt, and pepper in a bowl.
2. Add a little cooking oil or butter to a skillet that is already hot over medium heat.
3. Include the diced onions and bell peppers in the skillet. When they begin to soften, sauté.
4. Include the diced tomatoes and cooked Einkorn wheat berries in the skillet. Cook for a further 2 to 3 minutes.
5. Place the skillet with the remaining ingredients and the whisked eggs in it.
6. Gently stir the eggs as you cook them until they are scrambled, and the doneness you choose is reached.
7. Top the scramble with the shredded cheddar cheese, then put a lid on top to melt the cheese.
8. Remove the Einkorn breakfast scramble from the heat once the cheese has melted.

Einkorn Breakfast Omelette:

Ingredients:

- Two large eggs
- 1/4 cup cooked Einkorn wheat berries
- 1/4 cup diced bell peppers
- 1/4 cup diced onions
- 1/4 cup diced tomatoes
- 1/4 cup shredded cheddar cheese
- Salt and pepper to taste
- Cooking oil or butter for the skillet

Instructions:

1. Combine the eggs, salt, and pepper in a bowl.
2. Add a little cooking oil or butter to a skillet that is already hot over medium heat.

3. Include the diced onions and bell peppers in the skillet. When they begin to soften, sauté.
4. Include the diced tomatoes and cooked Einkorn wheat berries in the skillet. Cook for a further 2 to 3 minutes.
5. Place the skillet with the remaining ingredients and the whisked eggs in it.
6. Let the eggs boil until the edges begin to firm without stirring.
7. Cover one side of the omelet with the shredded cheddar cheese.
8. Carefully fold the omelet in half with a spatula once it is mostly set but is still a little runny.
9. Continue cooking for a further minute or until the cheese has melted and the omelet is fully cooked.
10. Place the hot Einkorn breakfast omelet on a platter.

Einkorn Breakfast Frittata:

Ingredients:
- Six large eggs
- 1/2 cup cooked Einkorn wheat berries
- 1/4 cup diced bell peppers
- 1/4 cup diced onions
- 1/4 cup diced tomatoes
- 1/4 cup shredded cheddar cheese
- Salt and pepper to taste
- Cooking oil or butter for the skillet

Instructions:
1. Set the oven's temperature to 350°F (175°C).
2. Combine the eggs, salt, and pepper in a bowl.
3. Heat a little butter or cooking oil in an ovenproof skillet over medium heat.

4. Include the diced onions and bell peppers in the skillet. When they begin to soften, sauté.
5. Include the diced tomatoes and cooked Einkorn wheat berries in the skillet. Cook for a further 2 to 3 minutes.
6. Place the skillet with the remaining ingredients and the whisked eggs in it.
7. Evenly cover the eggs with the shredded cheddar cheese.
8. On the burner, cook for a few minutes until the edges firm.
9. Place the skillet in the hot oven, and bake for 10 to 15 minutes, or until the frittata is set and just beginning to puff up.
10. Take the Einkorn breakfast frittata out of the oven, cool it briefly, and cut it into wedges. Serve warm.

Einkorn Breakfast Soufflé:

Ingredients:
- Four large eggs separated
- 1/4 cup cooked Einkorn wheat berries
- 1/4 cup diced bell peppers
- 1/4 cup diced onions
- 1/4 cup diced tomatoes
- 1/4 cup shredded cheddar cheese
- Salt and pepper to taste
- Cooking oil or butter for greasing

Instructions:
1. Set the oven's temperature to 350°F (175°C).
2. Combine the egg yolks, salt, and pepper in a bowl.
3. Add a little cooking oil or butter to a skillet that has been heated to medium heat.

4. Include the diced onions and bell peppers in the skillet. When they begin to soften, sauté.
5. Include the diced tomatoes and cooked Einkorn wheat berries in the skillet. Cook for a further 2 to 3 minutes.
6. Beat the egg whites in a different, clean, dry basin until firm peaks form.
7. Gently combine the beaten egg whites with the sautéed ingredients, shredded cheddar cheese, and egg yolks.
8. Spoon the mixture into an ovenproof dish that has been buttered.
9. Bake the soufflé in the oven for 20 to 25 minutes or until it puffs up and turns golden brown on top.
10. Take the Einkorn breakfast soufflé out of the oven while it's still fluffy, and serve it immediately.

Einkorn Breakfast Muffin:

Ingredients:

- 1 cup all-purpose Einkorn flour
- 1/2 cup cooked Einkorn wheat berries
- 1/4 cup diced ham or cooked breakfast sausage
- 1/4 cup diced bell peppers
- 1/4 cup diced onions
- 1/4 cup shredded cheddar cheese
- 1/4 cup milk
- 1/4 cup vegetable oil
- Two large eggs
- One teaspoon of baking powder
- Salt and pepper to taste

Instructions:

1. Grease or line a muffin pan with paper liners and preheat your oven to 375°F (190°C).
2. Combine the Einkorn flour, baking powder, salt, and pepper in a mixing dish.
3. Combine the eggs, milk, and vegetable oil in a separate bowl.
4. Combine the dry ingredients by adding the liquid components and stirring until mixed.
5. Stir in the shredded cheddar cheese, diced ham or sausage, cooked Einkorn wheat berries, diced bell peppers, and onions.
6. Evenly distribute the batter among the muffin tins.
7. Bake for 20 to 25 minutes in a preheated oven or until a toothpick inserted into the center of a muffin comes out clean.
8. After the Einkorn breakfast muffins have finished cooling in the muffin tray for a few minutes, move them to a wire rack to finish cooling.

Einkorn Breakfast Scone:

Ingredients:

- 2 cups all-purpose Einkorn flour
- 1/4 cup granulated sugar
- One tablespoon of baking powder
- 1/2 teaspoon salt
- 1/2 cup unsalted butter, cold and cubed
- 1/2 cup milk
- 1/2 cup cooked Einkorn wheat berries
- 1/4 cup diced dried fruits (e.g., cranberries, apricots)
- 1/4 cup chopped nuts (e.g., almonds, pecans)
- One teaspoon of vanilla extract

- One large egg, beaten (for egg wash)

Instructions:

1. Set your oven to 400 degrees Fahrenheit (200 degrees Celsius) and cover a baking sheet with parchment paper.
2. Combine the Einkorn flour, sugar, baking soda, and salt in a sizable mixing basin.
3. Combine the dry ingredients with the cooled, diced butter. Cut the butter into the flour mixture with a pastry cutter or fork until it resembles coarse crumbs.
4. Add the diced dried fruit, chopped almonds, and cooked Einkorn wheat berries.
5. Combine the milk and vanilla essence in a separate basin.
6. Add the liquid components to the dry ingredients and stir just until incorporated.
7. Spread the dough out onto a floured surface and give it a couple of gentle kneads to bring it together.
8. Form a 1-inch-thick circle out of the dough.
9. Cut the dough into eight wedges and arrange them on the baking sheet that has been prepared.
10. Brush some beaten egg on top to give the scones a golden sheen.
11. Bake the scones in the oven for 15 to 18 minutes or until golden brown.
12. Before serving, let the Einkorn breakfast scones cool on a wire rack.

Einkorn Breakfast Danish:

Ingredients:

For the Danish Pastry Dough:

- 1 1/4 cups all-purpose Einkorn flour
- 1/2 cup unsalted butter, cold and cubed
- 1/4 cup cold water
- 1/4 teaspoon salt
- One tablespoon sugar

For the Filling:

- 1/2 cup cream cheese
- 1/4 cup sugar
- One teaspoon of vanilla extract
- One egg yolk
- 1/2 cup fruit preserves (e.g., raspberry or apricot)
- 1/4 cup sliced almonds

For the Glaze:

- 1/2 cup powdered sugar
- 1-2 tablespoons milk
- 1/2 teaspoon vanilla extract

Instructions:

1. Combine the Einkorn flour, sugar, and salt in a mixing bowl. Add the cold, cubed butter and cut it into the flour with a pastry cutter or your fingertips until it resembles coarse crumbs.

2. When the dough begins to come together, add the cold water and stir. Refrigerate for 30 minutes after shaping it into a ball and wrapping it in plastic wrap.
3. Set a baking sheet on your stovetop and preheat your oven to 375°F (190°C).
4. Thoroughly combine the cream cheese, sugar, vanilla extract, and egg yolk in another dish. Place aside.
5. Roll out the cold dough into a sizable rectangle roughly 1/4 inch thick on a lightly dusted surface.
6. Make squares or rectangles out of the dough. Put a teaspoon of the fruit preserves and the cream cheese mixture in the middle of each square.
7. To create a triangle, fold the corners of each square over the filling. Using pressure, close the edges.
8. Arrange the danishes on the baking sheet that has been prepared, allowing space between them.
9. Scatter sliced almonds on top, and brush the tops with a little beaten egg.
10. Bake the danishes in the oven for 15 to 20 minutes or until golden brown.
11. Make the glaze while the danishes are baking. Combine powdered sugar, milk, and vanilla extract to make a smooth glaze.
12. Take the baked danishes out of the oven and allow them to cool for a moment. Over the top, drizzle the glaze.

Einkorn Breakfast Turnover:

Ingredients:

For the Turnover Pastry:

- 1 1/2 cups all-purpose Einkorn flour
- 1/2 cup unsalted butter, cold and cubed
- 1/4 cup cold water
- 1/4 teaspoon salt

For the Filling:

- 1 cup diced apples
- 1/4 cup brown sugar
- One teaspoon cinnamon
- 1/4 teaspoon nutmeg
- One tablespoon of lemon juice

For the Glaze:

- 1/2 cup powdered sugar
- 1-2 tablespoons milk
- 1/2 teaspoon vanilla extract

Instructions:

1. Make the pastry dough following the identical procedures outlined in the Danish recipe.
2. Combine chopped apples, brown sugar, cinnamon, nutmeg, and lemon juice in a mixing dish. Mix thoroughly.
3. Create a sizable rectangle out of the cold dough about 1/4 inch thick.

4. Divide the dough into rectangles or squares. Spread a spoonful of the apple filling

on the bottom half of each square.

5. Fold the remaining half of the dough over the filling to create a turnover. Using pressure, close the edges.
6. Arrange the turnovers on a parchment-lined baking sheet.
7. Bake at 375°F (190°C) in a preheated oven for 20 to 25 minutes or until golden brown.
8. Prepare the glaze by combining powdered sugar, milk, and vanilla essence while the turnovers are baking.
9. After the turnovers are finished, sprinkle the glaze on top, allowing them to cool somewhat.

Einkorn Breakfast Empanada:

Ingredients:

For the Empanada Dough:

- 2 cups all-purpose Einkorn flour
- 1/2 cup unsalted butter, cold and cubed
- 1/2 cup cold water
- One teaspoon salt

For the Filling:

- 1/2 pound ground sausage
- 1/2 cup diced bell peppers
- 1/4 cup diced onions
- 1/4 cup shredded cheddar cheese
- 1/4 teaspoon black pepper

- 1/4 teaspoon paprika
- 1/4 teaspoon cayenne pepper (optional)

Instructions:

1. To make the empanada dough, proceed as directed in the Danish recipe.
2. Brown the ground sausage in a pan over medium heat. Get rid of extra fat.
3. Include diced onions and bell peppers in the skillet. When they are soft, sauté.
4. Add black pepper, paprika, and cayenne pepper (if using) to the filling to season it.
5. Cut out circles from the refrigerated dough. Place a spoonful of the sausage and vegetable mixture on the inside of each circle. On top, sprinkle some cheddar cheese.
6. To create a half-moon shape, fold the remaining dough over the filling. Using pressure, close the edges.
7. Arrange the empanadas on a parchment-lined baking sheet.
8. Bake at 375°F (190°C) in a preheated oven for 20 to 25 minutes or until golden brown.

Einkorn Breakfast Calzone:

Ingredients:

For the Calzone Dough:

- 1 1/2 cups all-purpose Einkorn flour
- 1/2 teaspoon salt
- One teaspoon of active dry yeast
- 1/2 cup warm water
- One tablespoon of olive oil

For the Filling:

- 1/2 cup cooked breakfast sausage
- 1/2 cup scrambled eggs
- 1/4 cup diced bell peppers
- 1/4 cup diced onions
- 1/2 cup shredded mozzarella cheese
- Salt and pepper to taste

Instructions:

1. Combine Einkorn flour, salt, and active dry yeast in a bowl to make the calzone dough. Olive oil and warm water are added. Till the dough is smooth, knead it. For one hour, cover it and let it rise.
2. Set the oven's temperature to 450°F (230°C).
3. Separate the dough into small pieces and roll each piece into a round.
4. Arrange sausage, scrambled eggs, diced bell peppers, onions, and shredded mozzarella cheese on one side of each circle. Add salt and pepper to taste.
5. To create a half-moon shape, fold the remaining dough over the filling. Apply fork pressure to the edges to seal them.
6. Put the calzones on a baking sheet in step 6.
7. Bake in the oven for 15-20 minutes or until golden brown.

Einkorn Breakfast Stromboli:

Ingredients:

For the Stromboli Dough:

- 2 cups all-purpose Einkorn flour
- One packet (2 1/4 teaspoons) of active dry yeast
- 3/4 cup warm water
- One tablespoon of olive oil
- 1/2 teaspoon salt

For the Filling:

- 1/2 cup cooked breakfast sausage
- 1/2 cup diced ham
- 1/2 cup scrambled eggs
- 1/2 cup shredded cheddar cheese
- 1/4 cup diced bell peppers
- 1/4 cup diced onions
- Salt and pepper to taste

Instructions:

1. Combine Einkorn flour, active dry yeast, warm water, extra virgin olive oil, and salt to make the Stromboli dough in a bowl. Till the dough is smooth, knead it. For one hour, cover it and let it rise.
2. Set your oven's temperature to 400 °F (200 °C).
3. On a floured surface, roll out the dough into a rectangle.
4. Arrange the diced bell peppers, diced onions, cooked breakfast sausage, diced ham, scrambled eggs, and shredded cheddar cheese on the dough. Add salt and pepper to taste.

5. To form a log, tightly roll the dough, starting from one long side. To seal, pinch the edges.
6. Arrange the Stromboli on a parchment-lined baking pan.
7. Bake in the oven for 25 to 30 minutes or until golden brown.

Einkorn Breakfast Samosa:

Ingredients:

For the Samosa Dough:

- 2 cups all-purpose Einkorn flour
- 1/4 cup vegetable oil
- 1/2 teaspoon salt
- 1/2 cup water

For the Filling:

- 1 cup mashed potatoes
- 1/2 cup cooked breakfast sausage
- 1/4 cup frozen peas
- 1/4 cup diced onions
- One teaspoon cumin seeds
- One teaspoon of garam masala
- 1/2 teaspoon turmeric
- Salt and pepper to taste

Instructions:

1. Combine Einkorn flour, vegetable oil, salt, and water in a bowl to make the samosa dough. Till the dough is smooth, knead it. For 30 minutes, cover it and let it rest.
2. Add cumin seeds to hot oil in a skillet. Add the diced onions and cook them until transparent.

3. Include mashed potatoes, frozen peas, cooked breakfast sausage, garam masala, turmeric, salt, and pepper. Cook the ingredients until it is thoroughly cooked and mixed.
4. Set the oven's temperature to 375°F (190°C).
5. Cut circles from the rolled-out dough. To make semicircles, divide each circle in half.
6. Fold a semicircle of dough into a cone shape, moistening the edge to seal it.
7. Put the morning sausage and potato mixture inside the cone.
8. Fold the dough over and press to seal the open end of the samosa.
9. Arrange the samosas on a parchment-lined baking pan.
10. Bake in the oven for 20 to 25 minutes or until golden brown.

Einkorn Breakfast Pasty:

Ingredients:

For the Pasty Dough:

- 2 cups all-purpose Einkorn flour
- 1/2 cup unsalted butter, cold and cubed
- 1/2 cup cold water
- 1/2 teaspoon salt

For the Filling:

- 1/2 cup ground breakfast sausage
- 1/2 cup diced potatoes
- 1/4 cup diced onions

- 1/4 cup diced carrots
- Salt and pepper to taste
- One egg (for egg wash)

Instructions:

1. Make the pasty dough by following the Calzone recipe's instructions.
2. Brown the ground morning sausage in a pan over medium heat. Get rid of extra fat.
3. Fill the skillet with diced potatoes, onions, and carrots. When they are soft, sauté. Add salt and pepper to taste.
4. Set the oven's temperature to 375°F (190°C).
5. After cutting the dough into rounds, roll it out.
6. Distribute a spoonful of the sausage and veggie mixture on each circle's bottom half.
7. Create a half-moon shape by folding the remaining dough over the filling. Using pressure, close the edges.
8. Brush each pasty with an egg that has been beaten.
9. Arrange the pasties on a parchment-lined baking sheet.
10. Bake in a preheated oven for 25 to 30 minutes or until golden brown.

Einkorn Breakfast Dumplings:

Ingredients:

For the Dumplings:

- 1 cup all-purpose Einkorn flour
- One teaspoon of baking powder
- 1/2 teaspoon salt
- 1/2 cup milk

For the Breakfast Gravy:

- 1/2 cup cooked breakfast sausage
- Two tablespoons butter
- Two tablespoons of all-purpose Einkorn flour
- 1 1/2 cups milk
- Salt and pepper to taste

Instructions:

1. Combine Einkorn flour, baking soda, and salt in a mixing dish. Until you have a sticky dough, gradually add the milk.
2. Brown the morning sausage in a pan over medium heat. Sausage should be taken out of the skillet and put aside.
3. Melt butter in the same skillet over medium heat. To make a roux, add Einkorn flour and stir.
4. Stir in the milk gradually to create a creamy gravy. Add salt and pepper to taste. Re-heat the sausage in the skillet once it has been cooked.
5. Drop spoonfuls of dough into the simmering gravy to make the dumplings. The dumplings must be cooked and fluffy for 10 to 15 minutes while covered in a simmering liquid.

Einkorn Breakfast Poutine:

Ingredients:

For the Breakfast Gravy:

- Two tablespoons butter
- Two tablespoons of all-purpose Einkorn flour
- 1 1/2 cups milk
- Salt and pepper to taste
- 1/2 cup cooked breakfast sausage

For the Poutine:

- 2 cups frozen French fries
- 1 cup shredded cheddar cheese
- Two eggs, fried sunny-side-up

Instructions:

1. To make the breakfast gravy, prepare it in the same manner as for the dumplings, adding the cooked breakfast sausage afterward.
2. Prepare the frozen French fries as directed on the package until they are crisp while preparing the gravy.
3. In another skillet, cook the eggs sunny-side-up.
4. To assemble, arrange a platter with a serving of hot French fries. Cheddar cheese is shredded over the fries.
5. Drizzle the cheese and fries with the hot morning sausage gravy.
6. Add the sunny-side-up fried eggs to the poutine.

Einkorn Breakfast Nachos:

Ingredients:

- One bag (about 10 ounces) tortilla chips
- 1 cup cooked breakfast sausage
- 1 cup shredded cheddar cheese
- 1/4 cup diced tomatoes
- 1/4 cup diced bell peppers
- 1/4 cup sliced black olives
- 1/4 cup sliced green onions
- 1/4 cup sour cream

- Salsa, for serving (optional)

Instructions:

1. Set the oven's temperature to 350°F (175°C).
2. On a baking sheet, spread the tortilla chips uniformly.
3. Top the chips with shredded cheddar cheese and fried breakfast sausage.
4. On top of the cheese, scatter chopped tomatoes, bell peppers, black olives, and green onions.
5. Bake for 10 to 15 minutes in the oven until the cheese is melted and the nachos are thoroughly heated.
6. Take the dish out of the oven and top with sour cream. If desired, serve with salsa on the side.

Einkorn Breakfast Burrito Bowl:

Ingredients:

For the Burrito Bowl:

- 1 cup cooked Einkorn wheat berries
- 1/2 cup cooked breakfast sausage
- 1/4 cup diced bell peppers
- 1/4 cup diced onions
- 1/4 cup diced tomatoes
- 1/4 cup shredded cheddar cheese
- Two eggs scrambled
- Salt and pepper to taste
- Salsa, for serving

1. Arrange cooked Einkorn wheat berries, breakfast sausage, chopped tomatoes, diced bell peppers, and cheddar cheese in a bowl.
2. Scramble the eggs, add salt and pepper, and boil them in another bowl.
3. Add the scrambled eggs on top of the bowl.
4. Arrange the breakfast burrito bowl on a plate and serve with salsa.

Einkorn Breakfast Pizza Roll:

Ingredients:

For the Pizza Dough:

- 1 1/2 cups all-purpose Einkorn flour
- 1/2 teaspoon salt
- One packet (2 1/4 teaspoons) of active dry yeast
- 1/2 cup warm water
- One tablespoon of olive oil

For the Toppings:

- 1/2 cup cooked breakfast sausage
- 1/2 cup diced bell peppers
- 1/4 cup diced onions
- 1/2 cup shredded mozzarella cheese
- 1/4 cup pizza sauce

Instructions:

1. Combine Einkorn flour, salt, and active dry yeast in a bowl to make the pizza dough. Olive oil and warm water

are added. Till the dough is smooth, knead it. For one hour, cover it and let it rise.
2. Set the oven's temperature to 450°F (230°C).
3. Form a rectangle out of the rolled-out dough.
4. Leaving a border around the borders, evenly spread pizza sauce over the dough.
5. Arrange shredded mozzarella cheese, diced bell peppers, diced onions, and cooked breakfast sausage on top of the sauce.
6. Starting with one long side, tightly roll the dough up.
7. Lay the pizza roll seam-side down on a baking sheet covered with parchment paper.
8. Bake for 15 to 20 minutes in a preheated oven or until the cheese bubbles and the crust golden brown.

Einkorn Breakfast Taco Bowl:

Ingredients:

For the Taco Bowl:

- 1 cup cooked Einkorn wheat berries
- 1/2 cup cooked breakfast sausage
- 1/4 cup diced tomatoes
- 1/4 cup diced bell peppers
- 1/4 cup diced onions
- 1/4 cup shredded cheddar cheese
- Two eggs scrambled
- Salt and pepper to taste
- Salsa, sour cream, and sliced avocado for serving (optional)

Instructions:

1. Arrange cooked Einkorn wheat berries, breakfast sausage, diced tomatoes, bell peppers, onions, and cheddar cheese in a bowl.
2. Scramble the eggs, add salt and pepper, and boil them in another bowl.
3. Add the scrambled eggs on top of the taco bowl.
4. If you want, serve the breakfast taco bowl with sliced avocado, salsa, and sour cream on the side

Einkorn Breakfast Salad:

Ingredients:

For the Salad:

- 4 cups mixed greens (e.g., lettuce, spinach)
- 1 cup diced cooked bacon
- 1 cup diced hard-boiled eggs
- 1/2 cup diced tomatoes
- 1/4 cup diced red onions
- 1/4 cup shredded cheddar cheese

For the Dressing:

- 1/4 cup mayonnaise
- Two tablespoons sour cream
- Two tablespoons milk
- One teaspoon of Dijon mustard
- One teaspoon honey
- Salt and pepper to taste

Instructions:

1. Combine mixed greens, diced bacon, hard-boiled eggs, tomatoes, red onions, and shredded cheddar cheese in a big salad dish.
2. To create the dressing, combine the mayonnaise, sour cream, milk, honey, Dijon mustard, salt, and pepper in a separate bowl.
3. Drizzle the salad with the dressing and toss to coat thoroughly.
4. Immediately serve your Einkorn Breakfast Salad.

Einkorn Breakfast Grain Bowl:

Ingredients:

For the Grain Bowl:

- 1 cup cooked Einkorn wheat berries
- 1/2 cup diced cooked ham
- 1/4 cup diced bell peppers
- 1/4 cup diced onions
- 1/4 cup diced cucumbers
- 1/4 cup diced tomatoes
- Two hard-boiled eggs, sliced
- Salt and pepper to taste

For the Dressing:

- Two tablespoons of olive oil
- One tablespoon of balsamic vinegar
- One teaspoon honey
- 1/2 teaspoon Dijon mustard
- Salt and pepper to taste

Instructions:

1. Place cooked Einkorn wheat berries in a bowl with diced ham, bell peppers, onions, cucumbers, tomatoes, and hard-boiled eggs.
2. To make the dressing, combine the olive oil, balsamic vinegar, honey, Dijon mustard, salt, and pepper in a separate bowl.
3. Pour the dressing over the grain bowl and stir to evenly coat the ingredients.
4. Immediately serve your Einkorn Breakfast Grain Bowl.

Einkorn Breakfast Power Bowl:

Ingredients:

For the Power Bowl:

- 1 cup cooked Einkorn wheat berries
- 1/2 cup Greek yogurt
- 1/4 cup mixed berries (e.g., strawberries, blueberries, raspberries)
- 1/4 cup chopped nuts (e.g., almonds, walnuts)
- One tablespoon honey
- One tablespoon of chia seeds
- 1/2 teaspoon vanilla extract

Instructions:

1. Combine cooked Einkorn wheat berries, Greek yogurt, mixed berries, and finely chopped almonds in a bowl.
2. Scatter chia seeds on top and sprinkle honey over them.
3. Add a minimal amount of vanilla extract.
4. Once all the ingredients have been combined, serve the Einkorn Breakfast Power Bowl.

Einkorn Breakfast Buddha Bowl:

Ingredients:

For the Buddha Bowl:

- 1 cup cooked Einkorn wheat berries
- 1/2 cup diced avocado
- 1/4 cup diced cucumber
- 1/4 cup shredded carrots
- 1/4 cup diced red cabbage
- 1/4 cup chickpeas (canned, drained, and rinsed)
- Two tablespoons of tahini sauce
- One tablespoon of lemon juice
- Salt and pepper to taste
- Sesame seeds for garnish (optional)

Instructions:

1. Arrange cooked Einkorn wheat berries, diced cucumber, red cabbage, red avocado, and chickpeas in a bowl.
2. Combine the tahini sauce, lemon juice, salt, and pepper in a separate small bowl to make the dressing.
3. Drizzle the Buddha bowl with the dressing.
4. If desired, add sesame seeds as a garnish.
5. Immediately serve your Einkorn Breakfast Buddha Bowl.

Einkorn Breakfast Poke Bowl:

Ingredients:

For the Poke Bowl:

- 1 cup cooked Einkorn wheat berries

- 1/2 cup diced cooked salmon or tuna (sushi-grade)
- 1/4 cup diced cucumber
- 1/4 cup diced avocado
- 1/4 cup shredded carrots
- 1/4 cup seaweed salad (store-bought or homemade)
- Soy sauce or tamari for drizzling
- Sriracha mayo for drizzling (optional)
- Sesame seeds for garnish (optional)

Instructions:

1. Combine seaweed salad, sliced cucumber, diced avocado, shredded carrots, and cooked Einkorn wheat berries in a bowl.
2. To add flavor, drizzle with soy or tamari.
3. Drizzle with Sriracha Mayo (tune to your spice level) if you enjoy a little heat.
4. If desired, add sesame seeds as a garnish.
5. Immediately serve your Einkorn Breakfast Poke Bowl.

Einkorn Breakfast Smoothie Bowl:

Ingredients:

For the Smoothie Bowl:

- 1 cup frozen mixed berries (e.g., strawberries, blueberries, raspberries)
- 1/2 cup Greek yogurt
- 1/4 cup almond milk (or any milk of your choice)
- One tablespoon honey
- One banana, sliced
- Two tablespoons granola
- Fresh berries and sliced banana for topping

Instructions:

1. Blend frozen mixed berries, Greek yogurt, almond milk, and honey in a blender. Until smooth, blend.
2. Place a bowl with the smoothie inside.
3. Add fresh berries, granola, and banana slices to the smoothie's top.
4. Immediately serve your Einkorn Breakfast Smoothie Bowl.

Einkorn Breakfast Acai Bowl:

Ingredients:

For the Acai Bowl:

- One packet of frozen acai puree (unsweetened)
- 1/2 cup frozen mixed berries (e.g., strawberries, blueberries, raspberries)
- 1/2 banana
- 1/4 cup almond milk (or any milk of your choice)
- One tablespoon honey
- Two tablespoons granola
- Sliced banana and fresh berries for topping

Instructions:

1. Blend the frozen acai puree, mixed berries, almond milk, honey, and half a banana in a blender. Until smooth, blend.
2. Place the bowl with the acai mixture in it.
3. Add granola, banana slices, and fresh berries to the acai bowl as garnishes.
4. Immediately serve your Einkorn Breakfast Acai Bowl.

Einkorn Breakfast Danish:

Ingredients:

For the Danish Pastry Dough:

- 1 1/4 cups all-purpose Einkorn flour
- 1/2 cup unsalted butter, cold and cubed
- 1/4 cup cold water
- 1/4 teaspoon salt
- One tablespoon sugar

For the Filling:

- 1/2 cup cream cheese
- 1/4 cup sugar
- One teaspoon of vanilla extract
- One egg yolk
- 1/2 cup fruit preserves (e.g., raspberry or apricot)
- 1/4 cup sliced almonds

For the Glaze:

- 1/2 cup powdered sugar
- 1-2 tablespoons milk
- 1/2 teaspoon vanilla extract

Instructions:

1. Combine the Einkorn flour, sugar, and salt in a mixing bowl. Add the cold, cubed butter and cut it into the flour with a pastry cutter or your fingertips until it resembles coarse crumbs.
2. When the dough begins to come together, add the cold water and stir. Refrigerate for 30 minutes after shaping it into a ball and wrapping it in plastic wrap.

3. Set a baking sheet on your stovetop and preheat your oven to 375°F (190°C).
4. Thoroughly combine the cream cheese, sugar, vanilla extract, and egg yolk in another dish. Place aside.
5. Roll out the cold dough into a sizable rectangle roughly 1/4 inch thick on a lightly dusted surface.
6. Make squares or rectangles out of the dough. Put a teaspoon of the fruit preserves and the cream cheese mixture in the middle of each square.
7. To create a triangle, fold the corners of each square over the filling. Using pressure, close the edges.
8. Arrange the danishes on the baking sheet that has been prepared, allowing space between them.
9. Scatter sliced almonds on top, and brush the tops with a little beaten egg.
10. Bake the danishes in the oven for 15 to 20 minutes or until golden brown.
11. Make the glaze while the danishes are baking. Combine powdered sugar, milk, and vanilla extract to make a smooth glaze.
12. Take the baked danishes out of the oven and allow them to cool for a moment. Over the top, drizzle the glaze.

Einkorn Breakfast Turnover:

Ingredients:

For the Turnover Pastry:

- 1 1/2 cups all-purpose Einkorn flour
- 1/2 cup unsalted butter, cold and cubed
- 1/4 cup cold water
- 1/4 teaspoon salt

For the Filling:

- 1 cup diced apples
- 1/4 cup brown sugar
- One teaspoon cinnamon
- 1/4 teaspoon nutmeg
- One tablespoon of lemon juice

For the Glaze:

- 1/2 cup powdered sugar
- 1-2 tablespoons milk
- 1/2 teaspoon vanilla extract

Instructions:

1. Make the pastry dough following the identical procedures outlined in the Danish recipe.
2. Combine chopped apples, brown sugar, cinnamon, nutmeg, and lemon juice in a mixing dish. Mix thoroughly.
3. Create a sizable rectangle out of the cold dough about 1/4 inch thick.
4. Divide the dough into rectangles or squares. Spread a spoonful of the apple filling

on the bottom half of each square.

5. Fold the remaining half of the dough over the filling to create a turnover. Using pressure, close the edges.
6. Arrange the turnovers on a parchment-lined baking sheet.
7. Bake at 375°F (190°C) in a preheated oven for 20 to 25 minutes or until golden brown.
8. Prepare the glaze by combining powdered sugar, milk, and vanilla essence while the turnovers are baking.

9. After the turnovers are finished, sprinkle the glaze on top, allowing them to cool somewhat.

Einkorn Breakfast Empanada:

Ingredients:

For the Empanada Dough:

- 2 cups all-purpose Einkorn flour
- 1/2 cup unsalted butter, cold and cubed
- 1/2 cup cold water
- One teaspoon salt

For the Filling:

- 1/2 pound ground sausage
- 1/2 cup diced bell peppers
- 1/4 cup diced onions
- 1/4 cup shredded cheddar cheese
- 1/4 teaspoon black pepper
- 1/4 teaspoon paprika
- 1/4 teaspoon cayenne pepper (optional)

Instructions:

1. To make the empanada dough, proceed as directed in the Danish recipe.
2. Brown the ground sausage in a pan over medium heat. Get rid of extra fat.
3. Include diced onions and bell peppers in the skillet. When they are soft, sauté.
4. Add black pepper, paprika, and cayenne pepper (if using) to the filling to season it.

5. Cut out circles from the refrigerated dough. Place a spoonful of the sausage and vegetable mixture on the inside of each circle. On top, sprinkle some cheddar cheese.
6. To create a half-moon shape, fold the remaining dough over the filling. Using pressure, close the edges.
7. Arrange the empanadas on a parchment-lined baking sheet.
8. Bake at 375°F (190°C) in a preheated oven for 20 to 25 minutes or until golden brown.

Einkorn Breakfast Calzone:
Ingredients:

For the Calzone Dough:

- 1 1/2 cups all-purpose Einkorn flour
- 1/2 teaspoon salt
- One teaspoon of active dry yeast
- 1/2 cup warm water
- One tablespoon of olive oil

For the Filling:

- 1/2 cup cooked breakfast sausage
- 1/2 cup scrambled eggs
- 1/4 cup diced bell peppers
- 1/4 cup diced onions
- 1/2 cup shredded mozzarella cheese
- Salt and pepper to taste

Instructions:

1. Combine Einkorn flour, salt, and active dry yeast in a bowl to make the calzone dough. Olive oil and warm water are added. Till the dough is smooth, knead it. For one hour, cover it and let it rise.
2. Set the oven's temperature to 450°F (230°C).
3. Separate the dough into small pieces and roll each piece into a round.
4. Arrange sausage, scrambled eggs, diced bell peppers, onions, and shredded mozzarella cheese on one side of each circle. Add salt and pepper to taste.
5. To create a half-moon shape, fold the remaining dough over the filling. Apply fork pressure to the edges to seal them.
6. Put the calzones on a baking sheet in step 6.
7. Bake in the oven for 15-20 minutes or until golden brown.

Einkorn Breakfast Stromboli:

Ingredients:

For the Stromboli Dough:

- 2 cups all-purpose Einkorn flour
- One packet (2 1/4 teaspoons) of active dry yeast
- 3/4 cup warm water
- One tablespoon of olive oil
- 1/2 teaspoon salt

For the Filling:

- 1/2 cup cooked breakfast sausage
- 1/2 cup diced ham
- 1/2 cup scrambled eggs
- 1/2 cup shredded cheddar cheese
- 1/4 cup diced bell peppers
- 1/4 cup diced onions
- Salt and pepper to taste

Instructions:

1. Combine Einkorn flour, active dry yeast, warm water, extra virgin olive oil, and salt to make the Stromboli dough in a bowl. Till the dough is smooth, knead it. For one hour, cover it and let it rise.
2. Set your oven's temperature to 400 °F (200 °C).
3. On a floured surface, roll out the dough into a rectangle.
4. Arrange the diced bell peppers, diced onions, cooked breakfast sausage, diced ham, scrambled eggs, and shredded cheddar cheese on the dough. Add salt and pepper to taste.
5. To form a log, tightly roll the dough, starting from one long side. To seal, pinch the edges.
6. Arrange the Stromboli on a parchment-lined baking pan.
7. Bake in the oven for 25 to 30 minutes or until golden brown.

Einkorn Breakfast Samosa:

Ingredients:

For the Samosa Dough:

- 2 cups all-purpose Einkorn flour

- 1/4 cup vegetable oil
- 1/2 teaspoon salt
- 1/2 cup water

For the Filling:

- 1 cup mashed potatoes
- 1/2 cup cooked breakfast sausage
- 1/4 cup frozen peas
- 1/4 cup diced onions
- One teaspoon cumin seeds
- One teaspoon of garam masala
- 1/2 teaspoon turmeric
- Salt and pepper to taste

Instructions:

1. Combine Einkorn flour, vegetable oil, salt, and water in a bowl to make the samosa dough. Till the dough is smooth, knead it. For 30 minutes, cover it and let it rest.
2. Add cumin seeds to hot oil in a skillet. Add the diced onions and cook them until transparent.
3. Include mashed potatoes, frozen peas, cooked breakfast sausage, garam masala, turmeric, salt, and pepper. Cook the ingredients until it is thoroughly cooked and mixed.
4. Set the oven's temperature to 375°F (190°C).
5. Cut circles from the rolled-out dough. To make semicircles, divide each circle in half.
6. Fold a semicircle of dough into a cone shape, moistening the edge to seal it.
7. Put the morning sausage and potato mixture inside the cone.
8. Fold the dough over and press to seal the open end of the samosa.
9. Arrange the samosas on a parchment-lined baking pan.

10. Bake in the oven for 20 to 25 minutes or until golden brown.

Einkorn Breakfast Pasty:

Ingredients:

For the Pasty Dough:

- 2 cups all-purpose Einkorn flour
- 1/2 cup unsalted butter, cold and cubed
- 1/2 cup cold water
- 1/2 teaspoon salt

For the Filling:

- 1/2 cup ground breakfast sausage
- 1/2 cup diced potatoes
- 1/4 cup diced onions
- 1/4 cup diced carrots
- Salt and pepper to taste
- One egg (for egg wash)

Instructions:

1. Make the pasty dough by following the Calzone recipe's instructions.
2. Brown the ground morning sausage in a pan over medium heat. Get rid of extra fat.
3. Fill the skillet with diced potatoes, onions, and carrots. When they are soft, sauté. Add salt and pepper to taste.
4. Set the oven's temperature to 375°F (190°C).
5. After cutting the dough into rounds, roll it out.

6. Distribute a spoonful of the sausage and veggie mixture on each circle's bottom half.
7. Create a half-moon shape by folding the remaining dough over the filling. Using pressure, close the edges.
8. Brush each pasty with an egg that has been beaten.
9. Arrange the pasties on a parchment-lined baking sheet.
10. Bake in a preheated oven for 25 to 30 minutes or until golden brown.

Einkorn Breakfast Dumplings:

Ingredients:

For the Dumplings:

- 1 cup all-purpose Einkorn flour
- One teaspoon of baking powder
- 1/2 teaspoon salt
- 1/2 cup milk

For the Breakfast Gravy:

- 1/2 cup cooked breakfast sausage
- Two tablespoons butter
- Two tablespoons of all-purpose Einkorn flour
- 1 1/2 cups milk
- Salt and pepper to taste

Instructions:

1. Combine Einkorn flour, baking soda, and salt in a mixing dish. Until you have a sticky dough, gradually add the milk.
2. Brown the morning sausage in a pan over medium heat. Sausage should be taken out of the skillet and put aside.

3. Melt butter in the same skillet over medium heat. To make a roux, add Einkorn flour and stir.
4. Stir in the milk gradually to create a creamy gravy. Add salt and pepper to taste. Re-heat the sausage in the skillet once it has been cooked.
5. Drop spoonfuls of dough into the simmering gravy to make the dumplings. The dumplings must be cooked and fluffy for 10 to 15 minutes while covered in a simmering liquid.

Einkorn Breakfast Poutine:

Ingredients:

For the Breakfast Gravy:

- Two tablespoons butter
- Two tablespoons of all-purpose Einkorn flour
- 1 1/2 cups milk
- Salt and pepper to taste
- 1/2 cup cooked breakfast sausage

For the Poutine:

- 2 cups frozen French fries
- 1 cup shredded cheddar cheese
- Two eggs, fried sunny-side-up

Instructions:

1. To make the breakfast gravy, prepare it in the same manner as for the dumplings, adding the cooked breakfast sausage afterward.

2. Prepare the frozen French fries as directed on the package until they are crisp while preparing the gravy.
3. In another skillet, cook the eggs sunny-side-up.
4. To assemble, arrange a platter with a serving of hot French fries. Cheddar cheese is shredded over the fries.
5. Drizzle the cheese and fries with the hot morning sausage gravy.
6. Add the sunny-side-up fried eggs to the poutine.

Einkorn Breakfast Nachos:

Ingredients:
- One bag (about 10 ounces) tortilla chips
- 1 cup cooked breakfast sausage
- 1 cup shredded cheddar cheese
- 1/4 cup diced tomatoes
- 1/4 cup diced bell peppers
- 1/4 cup sliced black olives
- 1/4 cup sliced green onions
- 1/4 cup sour cream
- Salsa, for serving (optional)

Instructions:
1. Set the oven's temperature to 350°F (175°C).
2. On a baking sheet, spread the tortilla chips uniformly.
3. Top the chips with shredded cheddar cheese and fried breakfast sausage.
4. On top of the cheese, scatter chopped tomatoes, bell peppers, black olives, and green onions.
5. Bake for 10 to 15 minutes in the oven until the cheese is melted and the nachos are thoroughly heated.
6. Take the dish out of the oven and top with sour cream. If desired, serve with salsa on the side.

Einkorn Breakfast Burrito Bowl:

Ingredients:

For the Burrito Bowl:

- 1 cup cooked Einkorn wheat berries
- 1/2 cup cooked breakfast sausage
- 1/4 cup diced bell peppers
- 1/4 cup diced onions
- 1/4 cup diced tomatoes
- 1/4 cup shredded cheddar cheese
- Two eggs scrambled
- Salt and pepper to taste
- Salsa, for serving

Instructions:

1. Arrange cooked Einkorn wheat berries, breakfast sausage, chopped tomatoes, diced bell peppers, and cheddar cheese in a bowl.
2. Scramble the eggs, add salt and pepper, and boil them in another bowl.
3. Add the scrambled eggs on top of the bowl.
4. Arrange the breakfast burrito bowl on a plate and serve with salsa.

Einkorn Breakfast Pizza Roll:

Ingredients:

For the Pizza Dough:

- 1 1/2 cups all-purpose Einkorn flour
- 1/2 teaspoon salt
- One packet (2 1/4 teaspoons) of active dry yeast
- 1/2 cup warm water
- One tablespoon of olive oil

For the Toppings:

- 1/2 cup cooked breakfast sausage
- 1/2 cup diced bell peppers
- 1/4 cup diced onions
- 1/2 cup shredded mozzarella cheese
- 1/4 cup pizza sauce

Instructions:

1. Combine Einkorn flour, salt, and active dry yeast in a bowl to make the pizza dough. Olive oil and warm water are added. Till the dough is smooth, knead it. For one hour, cover it and let it rise.
2. Set the oven's temperature to 450°F (230°C).
3. Form a rectangle out of the rolled-out dough.
4. Leaving a border around the borders, evenly spread pizza sauce over the dough.
5. Arrange shredded mozzarella cheese, diced bell peppers, diced onions, and cooked breakfast sausage on top of the sauce.
6. Starting with one long side, tightly roll the dough up.

7. Lay the pizza roll seam-side down on a baking sheet covered with parchment paper.
8. Bake for 15 to 20 minutes in a preheated oven or until the cheese bubbles and the crust golden brown.

Einkorn Breakfast Taco Bowl:

Ingredients:

For the Taco Bowl:

- 1 cup cooked Einkorn wheat berries
- 1/2 cup cooked breakfast sausage
- 1/4 cup diced tomatoes
- 1/4 cup diced bell peppers
- 1/4 cup diced onions
- 1/4 cup shredded cheddar cheese
- Two eggs scrambled
- Salt and pepper to taste
- Salsa, sour cream, and sliced avocado for serving (optional)

Instructions:

1. Arrange cooked Einkorn wheat berries, breakfast sausage, diced tomatoes, bell peppers, onions, and cheddar cheese in a bowl.
2. Scramble the eggs, add salt and pepper, and boil them in another bowl.
3. Add the scrambled eggs on top of the taco bowl.
4. If you want, serve the breakfast taco bowl with sliced avocado, salsa, and sour cream on the side.

Einkorn Breakfast Salad:

Ingredients:

For the Salad:

- 4 cups mixed greens (e.g., lettuce, spinach)
- 1 cup diced cooked bacon
- 1 cup diced hard-boiled eggs
- 1/2 cup diced tomatoes
- 1/4 cup diced red onions
- 1/4 cup shredded cheddar cheese

For the Dressing:

- 1/4 cup mayonnaise
- Two tablespoons sour cream
- Two tablespoons milk
- One teaspoon of Dijon mustard
- One teaspoon honey
- Salt and pepper to taste

Instructions:

1. Mix mixed greens, diced bacon, hard-boiled eggs, tomatoes, red onions, and shredded cheddar cheese

in a large salad bowl.

2. Mix the mayonnaise, sour cream, milk, honey, Dijon mustard, salt, and pepper in a separate bowl to make the dressing.
3. Pour the dressing over the salad and toss to evenly coat.
4. Present your Einkorn Breakfast Salad right away.

Einkorn Breakfast Grain Bowl:

Ingredients:

For the Grain Bowl:

- 1 cup cooked Einkorn wheat berries
- 1/2 cup diced cooked ham
- 1/4 cup diced bell peppers
- 1/4 cup diced onions
- 1/4 cup diced cucumbers
- 1/4 cup diced tomatoes
- Two hard-boiled eggs, sliced
- Salt and pepper to taste

For the Dressing:

- Two tablespoons of olive oil
- One tablespoon of balsamic vinegar
- One teaspoon honey
- 1/2 teaspoon Dijon mustard
- Salt and pepper to taste

Instructions:

1. Place cooked Einkorn wheat berries in a bowl with diced ham, bell peppers, onions, cucumbers, tomatoes, and hard-boiled eggs.
2. To make the dressing, combine the olive oil, balsamic vinegar, honey, Dijon mustard, salt, and pepper in a separate small bowl.
3. Pour the dressing over the grain bowl and stir to evenly coat the ingredients.
4. Immediately serve your Einkorn Breakfast Grain Bowl.

Einkorn Breakfast Power Bowl:

Ingredients:

For the Power Bowl:

- 1 cup cooked Einkorn wheat berries
- 1/2 cup Greek yogurt
- 1/4 cup mixed berries (e.g., strawberries, blueberries, raspberries)
- 1/4 cup chopped nuts (e.g., almonds, walnuts)
- One tablespoon honey
- One tablespoon of chia seeds
- 1/2 teaspoon vanilla extract

Instructions:

1. Cooked Einkorn wheat berries, Greek yogurt, mixed berries, and chopped nuts should be arranged in a bowl.
2. Sprinkle chia seeds and drizzle honey on top.
3. Include a tiny bit of vanilla extract.
4. After combining all the ingredients, serve the Einkorn Breakfast Power Bowl.

Einkorn Breakfast Buddha Bowl:

Ingredients:

For the Buddha Bowl:

- 1 cup cooked Einkorn wheat berries
- 1/2 cup diced avocado
- 1/4 cup diced cucumber

- 1/4 cup shredded carrots
- 1/4 cup diced red cabbage
- 1/4 cup chickpeas (canned, drained, and rinsed)
- Two tablespoons of tahini sauce
- One tablespoon of lemon juice
- Salt and pepper to taste
- Sesame seeds for garnish (optional)

Instructions:

1. Arrange cooked Einkorn wheat berries, diced cucumber, red cabbage, red avocado, and chickpeas in a bowl.
2. Combine the tahini sauce, lemon juice, salt, and pepper in a separate small bowl to make the dressing.
3. Drizzle the Buddha bowl with the dressing.
4. If desired, add sesame seeds as a garnish.
5. Immediately serve your Einkorn Breakfast Buddha Bowl.

Einkorn Breakfast Poke Bowl:

Ingredients:

For the Poke Bowl:

- 1 cup cooked Einkorn wheat berries
- 1/2 cup diced cooked salmon or tuna (sushi-grade)
- 1/4 cup diced cucumber
- 1/4 cup diced avocado
- 1/4 cup shredded carrots
- 1/4 cup seaweed salad (store-bought or homemade)
- Soy sauce or tamari for drizzling
- Sriracha mayo for drizzling (optional)
- Sesame seeds for garnish (optional)

Instructions:
1. Combine seaweed salad, sliced cucumber, diced avocado, shredded carrots, and cooked Einkorn wheat berries in a bowl.
2. To add flavor, drizzle with soy or tamari.
3. Drizzle with Sriracha Mayo (tune to your spice level) if you enjoy a little heat.
4. If desired, add sesame seeds as a garnish.
5. Immediately serve your Einkorn Breakfast Poke Bowl.

Einkorn Breakfast Smoothie Bowl:

Ingredients:

For the Smoothie Bowl:

- 1 cup frozen mixed berries (e.g., strawberries, blueberries, raspberries)
- 1/2 cup Greek yogurt
- 1/4 cup almond milk (or any milk of your choice)
- One tablespoon honey
- One banana, sliced
- Two tablespoons granola
- Fresh berries and sliced banana for topping

Instructions:
1. Blend frozen mixed berries, Greek yogurt, almond milk, and honey in a blender. Until smooth, blend.
2. Place a bowl with the smoothie inside.
3. Add fresh berries, granola, and banana slices to the smoothie's top.
4. Immediately serve your Einkorn Breakfast Smoothie Bowl.

Einkorn Breakfast Acai Bowl:

Ingredients:

For the Acai Bowl:

- One packet of frozen acai puree (unsweetened)
- 1/2 cup frozen mixed berries (e.g., strawberries, blueberries, raspberries)
- 1/2 banana
- 1/4 cup almond milk (or any milk of your choice)
- One tablespoon honey
- Two tablespoons granola
- Sliced banana and fresh berries for topping

Instructions:

1. Blend the frozen acai puree, mixed berries, almond milk, honey, and half a banana in a blender. Until smooth, blend.
2. Place the bowl with the acai mixture in it.
3. Add granola, banana slices, and fresh berries to the acai bowl as garnishes.
4. Immediately serve your Einkorn Breakfast Acai Bowl.

Einkorn Breakfast Chia Pudding:

Ingredients:

- 1/4 cup einkorn berries
- 1 cup almond milk (or your choice of milk)
- Two tablespoons chia seeds
- One tablespoon of honey or maple syrup (optional)
- Fresh berries or sliced fruit for topping

Instructions:

1. Use a blender or food processor to grind the einkorn berries into coarse flour.
2. Chia seeds, almond milk, einkorn flour, and sweetener (if used) should all be combined in a bowl.
3. Stir thoroughly, then chill for at least two hours or overnight.
4. Place fresh fruit on top of the dish.

Einkorn Breakfast Parfait:

Ingredients:

- 1/2 cup einkorn flakes
- 1 cup Greek yogurt
- 1/2 cup fresh berries
- Two tablespoons of honey or agave syrup
- 1/4 cup granola

Instructions:

1. Fill the bottom of a glass or jar with einkorn flakes.
2. Spread Greek yogurt on top.
3. Place fresh berries on top, then sprinkle honey or agave syrup.
4. If desired, repeat the layers.
5. Add some granola on top to finish.
6.

Einkorn Breakfast Yogurt Bowl:

Ingredients:

- 1 cup Greek yogurt
- 1/4 cup einkorn flakes
- 1/4 cup mixed nuts and dried fruits
- One tablespoon honey

- Sliced banana or berries for garnish

Instructions:
1. Greek yogurt should be added to a bowl.
2. Top the yogurt with chopped nuts or dried fruit and einkorn flakes.
3. Spoon honey over the top.
4. Add fruit slices as a garnish.

Einkorn Breakfast Granola:

Ingredients:
- 2 cups einkorn flakes
- 1/2 cup mixed nuts and seeds
- 1/4 cup honey or maple syrup
- Two tablespoons of coconut oil
- One teaspoon of vanilla extract
- 1/2 cup dried fruits (e.g., raisins, cranberries)

Instructions:
1. Set the oven's temperature to 325°F (163°C).
2. Combine einkorn flakes, almonds, and seeds in a big bowl.
3. Melt the honey and coconut oil in a small saucepan over low heat. Add vanilla extract and stir.
4. Add the honey mixture to the dry ingredients and well combine.
5. Evenly distribute the mixture on a baking sheet, then bake for 20 to 25 minutes, stirring once or twice, or until golden brown.
6. After the granola has cooled, combine the dried fruits.

Einkorn Breakfast Trail Mix:

Ingredients:

- 1 cup einkorn flakes
- 1/2 cup mixed nuts
- 1/2 cup dried fruits (e.g., apricots, cherries)
- 1/4 cup chocolate chips or dark chocolate chunks (optional)

Instructions:

5. In a dish, mix the einkorn flakes, mixed nuts, dried fruit, and chocolate (if using).
6. Mix well.
7. For a simple on-the-go snack, portion it into tiny bags or containers.

Einkorn Breakfast Energy Balls:

Ingredients:

- 1 cup einkorn flakes
- 1/2 cup nut butter (e.g., almond, peanut)
- 1/3 cup honey or maple syrup
- 1/2 cup shredded coconut
- 1/4 cup mini chocolate chips (optional)

Instructions:

5. Combine einkorn flakes, nut butter, honey, coconut shreds, and chocolate chips (if using) in a bowl.
6. The mixture should be formed into bite-sized balls.
7. To set, refrigerate for about 30 minutes.
8. Snack on it for a rapid energy boost.

Einkorn Breakfast Protein Bars:

Ingredients:

- 1 1/2 cups einkorn flakes
- 1 cup protein powder (flavor of your choice)
- 1/2 cup nut butter
- 1/3 cup honey or agave syrup
- 1/2 cup dried fruits (e.g., dates, apricots)
- 1/4 cup chopped nuts

Instructions:

1. Einkorn flakes, protein powder, nut butter, honey, dried fruit, and chopped nuts should all be combined in a mixing dish.
2. After pressing the mixture into a prepared pan, could you place it in the fridge for a few hours?
3. Cut the mixture into bars for a quick breakfast or snack and keep it in the refrigerator.

Einkorn Breakfast Muesli:

Ingredients:

- 1 cup einkorn flakes
- 1/2 cup rolled oats
- 1/4 cup chopped nuts
- 1/4 cup dried fruits (e.g., raisins, cranberries)
- One tablespoon of honey or maple syrup
- 1 cup yogurt or milk

Instructions:

1. Einkorn flakes, rolled oats, chopped almonds, and dried fruit should all be combined in a bowl.
2. Drizzle maple syrup or honey over the mixture.

3. Add milk or yogurt, stirring thoroughly after each addition.
4. Let it soften for a few minutes before consuming.

Einkorn Breakfast Overnight Oats:

Ingredients:

- 1/2 cup einkorn flakes
- 1/2 cup rolled oats
- 1 cup milk (dairy or non-dairy)
- One tablespoon of honey or maple syrup
- Fresh fruit or berries for topping

Instructions:

1. Combine einkorn flakes, rolled oats, milk, and sweeteners in a jar or other container.
2. Stir thoroughly, cover, and chill for the night.
3. Before serving, please stir it well in the morning and top it with fruit or berries.

Einkorn Breakfast Chia Popsicles:

Ingredients:

- 1/4 cup einkorn flour
- 1 1/2 cups milk (dairy or non-dairy)
- Two tablespoons chia seeds
- Two tablespoons of honey or agave syrup
- Sliced fruit (e.g., berries, kiwi)

Instructions:

1. Einkorn flour and milk should be thoroughly combined.
2. Pour the mixture into a bowl, then add the honey and chia seeds.

3. Pour mixture into popsicle molds and top with fruit slices.
4. Freeze for a minimum of four hours or until it is solid.

Einkorn Breakfast Fruit Salad:

Ingredients:

- Assorted fresh fruits (e.g., strawberries, pineapple, grapes)
- One tablespoon of honey or agave syrup (optional)
- Fresh mint leaves for garnish

Instructions:

1. Wash the fruits, then chop them into bite-sized pieces as part of preparation.
2. Combine the fruits in a bowl and, if preferred, drizzle with honey or agave nectar.
3. Use fresh mint leaves as a garnish.

Einkorn Breakfast Fruit Kabobs:

Ingredients:

- Assorted fresh fruits (e.g., melon, pineapple, berries)
- Wooden skewers

Instructions:

1. Wash the fresh fruits and chop them into bite-sized pieces.
2. Throw the fruit pieces onto the wooden skewers with whichever design you desire.
3. Use it as a bright and entertaining breakfast choice.

Einkorn Breakfast Fruit Platter:

Ingredients:

- A variety of fresh fruits (e.g., apple slices, grapes, citrus wedges)
- Optional: a drizzle of honey or yogurt for dipping

Instructions:

1. Place the fresh fruit in an appealing arrangement on a dish, and if desired, provide a small cup of honey or yogurt for dipping.

Einkorn Breakfast Fruit Pizza:

Ingredients:

- Einkorn pizza crust (premade or homemade)
- Greek yogurt or cream cheese (as a base)
- Sliced fresh fruits (e.g., kiwi, strawberries, banana)
- Honey for drizzling

Instructions:

1. Top the einkorn pizza dough with a layer of cream cheese or Greek yogurt.
2. The sliced fresh fruits should be arranged on top.
3. Pour honey on top of the fruit.
4. Cut and present.

Einkorn Breakfast Fruit Dip:

Ingredients:

- 1 cup Greek yogurt
- Two tablespoons honey
- 1/2 teaspoon vanilla extract

- Assorted fresh fruit for dipping (e.g., apple slices, berries)

Instructions:

1. Greek yogurt, honey, and vanilla essence should all be thoroughly blended in a bowl.
2. Offer fresh fruit on the side for dipping along with the fruit dip.
3.

Einkorn Breakfast Fruit Salsa:

Ingredients:

- Assorted fresh fruits (e.g., mango, pineapple, kiwi)
- One tablespoon of lime juice
- One tablespoon honey
- Fresh mint leaves for garnish

Instructions:

1. Chop the fresh fruit into uniformly sized cubes.
2. Combine lime juice, honey, and fruit.
3. Add fresh mint leaves as a garnish.

Einkorn Breakfast Fruit Smoothie:

Ingredients:

- Assorted fresh fruits (e.g., banana, berries, mango)
- Greek yogurt
- Milk (dairy or non-dairy)
- Honey (optional for sweetness)
- Ice cubes (optional)

Instructions:
1. Smoothly combine the milk, Greek yogurt, and fresh fruit in a blender.
2. If desired, add honey for sweetness.
3. Blend in ice cubes until the smoothie has the consistency you prefer.
4. Serve right away.

Einkorn Breakfast Fruit Sorbet:

Ingredients:
- Assorted frozen fruits (e.g., berries, peaches, pineapple)
- Greek yogurt or coconut milk (optional for creaminess)
- Honey or maple syrup (optional for sweetness)

Instructions:
1. The frozen fruits should be blended until they resemble sorbet. Add Greek yogurt or coconut milk for desired creaminess and honey or maple syrup for sweetness. As a cool breakfast treat, serve.

Einkorn Breakfast Fruit Parfait:

Ingredients:
- 1 cup Einkorn breakfast cereal
- 1 cup Greek yogurt
- 1 cup mixed fresh fruits (such as berries, sliced bananas, and kiwi)
- 1/4 cup honey or maple syrup (optional)
- 1/4 cup chopped nuts or granola (optional)
- Fresh mint leaves for garnish (optional)

Instructions:

1. Prepare your preferred fresh fruit first. When necessary, wash and cut them.
2. Combine the Greek yogurt and einkorn breakfast cereal in a bowl. You can taste-test, adding honey or maple syrup for a sweeter parfait.
3. Place your parfait in a bowl or serving glass and layer it. At the bottom, start with a spoonful of the yogurt-cereal mixture.
4. After placing a layer of yogurt-cereal on top, add a layer of mixed fresh fruits.
5. Continue adding layers until the glass or bowl is full. Yogurt-cereal and fruits can be alternated.
6. For some extra texture and crunch, if preferred, garnish with chopped nuts or granola.
7. To add sweetness and color, garnish with fresh mint leaves before adding a drizzle of honey or maple syrup.
8. Immediately serve your Einkorn Breakfast Fruit Parfait or store it in the fridge until you're ready to eat.

Einkorn Breakfast Fruit Yogurt:

Ingredients:

- 1 cup Einkorn breakfast cereal
- 1 cup Greek yogurt
- 1 cup mixed fresh fruits (such as berries, sliced bananas, and mango)
- 1/4 cup honey or maple syrup (optional)
- 1/4 cup chopped nuts (optional)

Instructions:

1. Combine Greek yogurt and Einkorn breakfast cereal in a bowl.
2. Adding honey or maple syrup will make the dish sweeter, so do so.
3. Sprinkle chopped nuts and various fresh fruits on top of the yogurt-cereal mixture.
4. Enjoy your Einkorn Fruit Yogurt for Breakfast.

Einkorn Breakfast Fruit Bowl:

Ingredients:

- 1 cup Einkorn breakfast cereal
- 1 cup mixed fresh fruits (e.g., berries, apple slices, and grapes)
- 1/4 cup chopped nuts (e.g., almonds or walnuts)
- 1/4 cup Greek yogurt (optional)
- One tablespoon honey (optional)

Instructions:

1. Fill a bowl with the Einkorn breakfast cereal.
2. Include the chopped nuts and other fresh fruits.
3. You can add a dollop of Greek yogurt and honey on top.
4. After combining everything, eat your Einkorn Breakfast Fruit Bowl.

Einkorn Breakfast Fruit Tray:

Ingredients:

- A variety of fresh fruits (e.g., strawberries, melon, grapes, and kiwi)
- Einkorn breakfast cereal (for serving)

Instructions:
1. As needed, wash, peel, and slice the fresh fruits.
2. Arrange the fruit slices on a sizable serving platter.
3. Put a bowl of einkorn cereal out on the tray.
4. Offer the cereal and fruit together, and let each person assemble their own Einkorn Breakfast Fruit Tray.

Einkorn Breakfast Fruit Board:

Ingredients:
- Assorted fresh fruits (e.g., berries, apple slices, and citrus segments)
- Einkorn breakfast cereal
- Greek yogurt
- Honey
- Nuts (e.g., almonds, walnuts)
- Dried fruits (e.g., raisins, apricots)

Instructions:
1. Arrange the fresh fruit, Greek yogurt, honey, nuts, einkorn breakfast cereal, and dried fruit on a sizable wooden board or platter.
2. Allow everyone to assemble their own Einkorn Breakfast Fruit Board by mixing and matching the ingredients.

Einkorn Breakfast Fruit Spread:

Ingredients:
- 1 cup Einkorn breakfast cereal
- 1/2 cup mixed fresh fruits (e.g., diced apples, berries)
- Two tablespoons of nut butter (e.g., almond or peanut butter)

- Honey or maple syrup for drizzling (optional)

Instructions:

1. Combine the Einkorn breakfast cereal with various fresh fruits in a bowl.
2. Lightly reheat the nut butter until it is drizzle-friendly.
3. Pour the nut butter over the fruit and cereal.
4. For extra sweetness, you can sprinkle on some honey or maple syrup.
5. After combining everything, have your Einkorn Breakfast Fruit Spread.

Einkorn Breakfast Fruit Bruschetta:

Ingredients:

- One baguette of rustic bread, sliced
- 1 cup Einkorn breakfast cereal
- 1 cup mixed fresh fruits (e.g., diced strawberries, kiwi, and pineapple)
- Honey or balsamic glaze for drizzling
- Fresh mint leaves for garnish

Instructions:

1. Toast the baguette or rustic bread slices until they are just beginning to get crunchy.
2. Combine the Einkorn breakfast cereal with various fresh fruits in a bowl.
3. Position the dish with the toasty bread slices.
4. Place a spoonful of the fruit-cereal mixture onto each slice.
5. Add a glaze made of honey or balsamic vinegar.
6. Add fresh mint leaves as a garnish.
7. Give your guests the Einkorn Breakfast Fruit Bruschetta as a tasty starter.

Einkorn Breakfast Fruit Nachos:

Ingredients:

- 1 cup Einkorn breakfast cereal
- 1 cup mixed fresh fruits (e.g., sliced bananas, strawberries, and blueberries)
- 1/2 cup Greek yogurt
- 1/4 cup honey
- 1/4 cup chopped nuts (e.g., almonds or pecans)
- Cinnamon for sprinkling (optional)

Instructions:

1. To create the "nacho" base, arrange the einkorn breakfast cereal on a serving tray.
2. Evenly distribute the fresh fruit mixture over the cereal.
3. Drizzle honey and Greek yogurt on top.
4. If desired, top with chopped nuts and a splash of cinnamon.
5. Offer guests your Einkorn Breakfast Fruit Nachos as a tasty and nutritious snack.

Einkorn Breakfast Fruit Tacos:

Ingredients:

- Small tortillas (corn or flour)
- 1 cup Einkorn breakfast cereal
- 1 cup mixed fresh fruits (e.g., diced mango, pineapple, and kiwi)
- Greek yogurt or coconut yogurt
- Honey or agave nectar for drizzling
- Shredded coconut (optional)

Instructions:
1. Heat the tortillas as directed on the package.
2. Place a scoop of Einkorn breakfast cereal and fresh fruits into each tortilla.
3. Drizzle with honey or agave nectar and Greek yogurt.
4. You can top it up with some shredded coconut.
5. Fold the tortillas and plate the fruit tacos made with Einkorn cereal.

Einkorn Breakfast Fruit Quesadilla:

Ingredients:
- Two small flour tortillas
- 1/2 cup Einkorn breakfast cereal
- 1/2 cup mixed fresh fruits (e.g., diced peaches, berries)
- 1/4 cup cream cheese or Greek yogurt
- Honey or powdered sugar for drizzling (optional)

Instructions:
1. Heat a skillet with one tortilla over medium heat.
2. Cover the tortilla with cream cheese or Greek yogurt.
3. It is evenly topped with assorted fresh fruits and Einkorn breakfast cereal.
4. To make a quesadilla, top with the second tortilla.
5. Cook until lightly browned and crisp, a couple of minutes on each side.
6. If preferred, sprinkle with powdered sugar or drizzle with honey.
7. Cut your Einkorn Breakfast Fruit Quesadilla into wedges and serve.

Einkorn Breakfast Fruit Burrito:

Ingredients:

- One large flour tortilla
- 1 cup Einkorn breakfast cereal
- 1 cup mixed fresh fruits (e.g., sliced strawberries, blueberries)
- 1/4 cup Greek yogurt
- One tablespoon honey
- Sliced almonds or chia seeds (optional)

Instructions:

1. The flour tortilla should be placed level on a tidy surface.
2. Cover the tortilla's middle with Greek yogurt.
3. Top the yogurt with mixed fresh fruits and Einkorn breakfast cereal.
4. Add honey to the dish.
5. At your discretion, you can add sliced almonds or chia seeds for further nutrition and crunch.
6. Fold the tortilla's sides inward and roll it up to make the Einkorn Breakfast Fruit Burrito.
7. If preferred, cut it in half and savor it.

Einkorn Breakfast Fruit Sushi:

Ingredients:

- 1 cup cooked and cooled Einkorn breakfast cereal (sticky consistency)
- Nori seaweed sheets
- Mixed fresh fruits (e.g., avocado, mango, cucumber)
- Low-sodium soy sauce or tamari (for dipping)

Instructions:
1. Place a plastic wrap sheet on a spotless surface.
2. Lay a sheet of nori seaweed over the plastic wrap.
3. Cover the nori sheet with a uniform layer of cooked einkorn cereal.
4. Top the cereal with strips of various fresh fruits (such as avocado, mango, and cucumber).
5. Shape the nori sheet into a sushi roll by firmly rolling it and using plastic wrap to help.
6. Cut the roll into small pieces.
7. Offer soy sauce or tamari as a dipping sauce with your Einkorn Breakfast Fruit Sushi.

Einkorn Breakfast Fruit Wraps:

Ingredients:
- Large whole wheat tortillas
- 1 cup Einkorn breakfast cereal
- 1 cup mixed fresh fruits (e.g., sliced peaches, berries)
- 1/4 cup almond or peanut butter
- Honey or agave nectar (optional)
- Sliced almonds (optional)

Instructions:
1. Spread a tortilla out on a spotless surface.
2. Cover the tortilla with a coating of almond or peanut butter.
3. Distribute evenly the mixed fresh fruits and Einkorn breakfast cereal.
4. If preferred, drizzle with honey or agave nectar.
5. You can add sliced almonds for more crunch if you like.
6. Tightly roll the tortilla, folding the sides in as you go.
7. Slice the Einkorn Breakfast Fruit Wraps in half or into smaller pieces and serve.

Einkorn Breakfast Fruit Roll-Ups:

Ingredients:

- 2 cups Einkorn breakfast cereal
- 1 cup mixed fresh fruits (e.g., mashed bananas, diced apples)
- Two tablespoons honey
- Parchment paper

Instructions:

1. To make the einkorn breakfast cereal sticky and smooth, combine it with the honey and mixed fresh fruits in a food processor.
2. Use parchment paper to cover a baking sheet.
3. Create a rectangle on the parchment paper by spreading the cereal-fruit mixture equally across it.
4. Lay another piece of parchment paper on top, then roll the mixture to the desired thickness.
5. Please take off the top parchment paper and allow it to dry for a few hours to harden and become malleable.
6. After the sheet has dried, cut it into strips and roll them up.
7. Take pleasure in your fruit roll-ups from Einkorn Breakfast as a portable snack.

Einkorn Breakfast Fruit Popsicles:

Ingredients:

- 2 cups Einkorn breakfast cereal
- 1 cup mixed fresh fruits (e.g., pureed strawberries, diced mango)
- 1 cup Greek yogurt
- Two tablespoons honey
- Popsicle molds and sticks

Instructions:

1. In a bowl, Thoroughly Einkorn breakfast cereal, Greek yogurt, and honey.
2. Fill pop in a bowlsicle mold with a layer of cereal-yogurt mixture and mixed fresh fruit.
3. Place popsicle sticks inside every mold.
4. Freeze for several hours or until solid.
5. Take out your Einkorn Breakfast Fruit Popsicles from the molds and enjoy.

Einkorn Breakfast Fruit Ice Cream:

Ingredients:

- 2 cups Einkorn breakfast cereal
- 2 cups mixed fresh fruits (e.g., frozen berries, banana slices)
- 1 cup Greek yogurt
- 1/4 cup honey or maple syrup
- One teaspoon of vanilla extract (optional)

Instructions:

1. Blend or process the Greek yogurt, honey, maple syrup, einkorn breakfast cereal, mixed fresh fruits, and vanilla extract (if using) until smooth.
2. Blend the mixture until it's creamy and smooth.
3. Spoon the mixture into an airtight container, then freeze it for at least 4 hours or until it has the consistency you prefer for ice cream.
4. Scoop your Einkorn Breakfast Fruit Ice Cream and serve it.

Einkorn Breakfast Fruit Galette:

Ingredients:

- One pre-made pie crust (store-bought or homemade)
- 2 cups mixed fresh fruits (e.g., sliced peaches, berries)
- 1/2 cup Einkorn breakfast cereal
- 1/4 cup granulated sugar
- One tablespoon of lemon juice
- One egg (for egg wash)
- Powdered sugar (for dusting, optional)
- Vanilla ice cream (for serving, optional)

Instructions:

1. Set the oven's temperature to 375°F (190°C).
2. Combine the Einkorn breakfast cereal, mixed fresh fruits, sugar, and lemon juice in a bowl.
3. On a baking sheet that has been lined with parchment paper, roll out the pie crust.
4. Spoon the fruit and cereal mixture over the pie crust's center, leaving a border around the edges.
5. Fold the pie crust's edges over the fruit, making any necessary pleats.
6. To give the borders of the galette a golden sheen, beat an egg and brush it over them.
7. Bake the dish for 30 to 35 minutes until the fruit is bubbling and the crust is brown.
8. Take it out of the oven, then cool a little before serving.
9. Serve with vanilla ice cream and, if wanted, dust with powdered sugar.

Einkorn Breakfast Fruit Tart:

Ingredients:

- One pre-made tart crust (store-bought or homemade)
- 1 1/2 cups einkorn breakfast cereal

- 1 1/2 cups mixed fresh fruits (e.g., sliced peaches, kiwi, and strawberries)
- 1/4 cup apricot jam or fruit preserves

Instructions:

1. Set the oven's temperature to 350°F (175°C).
2. Bake the tart crust following the directions on the package or the handmade recipe. Allow it to cool.
3. Place the einkorn breakfast cereal and various fresh fruits in a bowl.
4. Warm the apricot jam or fruit preserves in a saucepan until they are liquid.
5. Spread the jam over the tart crust that has cooled.
6. Spread the fruit and grain mixture over the crust coated in jam.
7. Place your Einkorn Breakfast Fruit Tart in the refrigerator for at least 30 minutes before serving.

Einkorn Breakfast Fruit Crisp:

Ingredients:

- 4 cups mixed fresh fruits (e.g., apples, pears, berries)
- 1 cup Einkorn breakfast cereal
- 1/2 cup rolled oats
- 1/4 cup all-purpose flour
- 1/4 cup brown sugar
- 1/4 cup unsalted butter, cold and cubed
- 1/2 teaspoon ground cinnamon
- Vanilla ice cream or whipped cream (for serving, optional)

Instructions:

1. Set the oven's temperature to 375°F (190°C).
2. As required, peel, core, and slice the fresh fruits.

3. Combine the mixed fresh fruits with one tablespoon of brown sugar, two tablespoons of Einkorn breakfast cereal, and a large bowl.
4. Spoon the fruit mixture into an oven-safe dish.
5. Combine the leftover einkorn cereal, rolled oats, flour, remaining brown sugar, cold cubed butter, and ground cinnamon in another bowl. Mix the ingredients with a pastry cutter or your fingertips until they resemble coarse crumbs.
6. Evenly sprinkle the fruit in the baking dish with the cereal-oat mixture.
7. Bake for 30-35 minutes or until the fruit bubbles and the topping is golden brown.
8. Allow it to cool a bit before serving.
9. Warm up your Einkorn Breakfast Fruit Crisp and serve it with optional whipped cream or vanilla ice cream on top.

Einkorn Breakfast Fruit Cobbler:

Ingredients:

- 4 cups mixed fresh fruits (e.g., peaches, berries, and plums)
- 1 cup Einkorn breakfast cereal
- 1/2 cup all-purpose flour
- 1/2 cup granulated sugar
- 1/4 cup unsalted butter, melted
- 1/2 cup milk
- One teaspoon of vanilla extract
- 1/2 teaspoon baking powder
- A pinch of salt
- Vanilla ice cream or whipped cream (for serving, optional)

Instructions:

1. Set the oven's temperature to 350°F (175°C).
2. Put a baking dish full of a variety of fresh fruits.
3. Combine the milk, vanilla essence, baking powder, einkorn breakfast cereal, all-purpose flour, granulated sugar, melted butter, and a dash of salt in a bowl.
4. Evenly distribute the cereal batter over the assortment of fresh fruits in the baking dish.
5. Bake for 35 to 40 minutes or until the fruit is bubbling and the topping is brown.
6. Let it cool just a little before serving.
7. Warm up your Einkorn Breakfast Fruit Cobbler and serve it with optional whipped cream or vanilla ice cream on top.

Einkorn Breakfast Fruit Trifle:

Ingredients:

- 2 cups Einkorn breakfast cereal
- 2 cups mixed fresh fruits (e.g., cubed pineapple, berries)
- 2 cups vanilla pudding (store-bought or homemade)
- Whipped cream
- Fresh mint leaves for garnish (optional)

Instructions:

1. Begin by piling einkorn breakfast cereal at the bottom of a trifle dish or individual serving glasses.
2. On top of the cereal, add a layer of assorted fresh fruits.
3. Top the fruit with a layer of vanilla pudding.
4. Continue layering until you reach the dish's or glass's top.
5. Add a dollop of whipped cream to the top and, if preferred, a few fresh mint leaves for decoration.
6. Present your fruit trifle with chilled Einkorn cereal.

Einkorn Breakfast Fruit Napoleon:

Ingredients:

For the pastry layers:

- One sheet of puff pastry
- One egg (for egg wash)
- One tablespoon water (for egg wash)
- One tablespoon powdered sugar (for dusting)

For the fruit filling:

- 2 cups of mixed berries (strawberries, blueberries, raspberries)
- Two tablespoons honey
- One teaspoon of lemon juice
- 1/2 teaspoon vanilla extract

For the whipped cream:

- 1 cup heavy cream
- Two tablespoons powdered sugar
- One teaspoon of vanilla extract

Instructions:

1. Set the oven's temperature to 375°F (190°C).
2. Roll out the puff pastry sheet into a sizable rectangle on a lightly dusted surface. Cut it into smaller rectangles, each measuring about 3 x 5 inches.
3. Arrange the pastry rectangles on a parchment-lined baking sheet. Brush an egg wash over the pastry rectangles by whisking together the egg and water.

4. Bake the pastry rectangles in the oven for 12 to 15 minutes or until they bubble up and turn golden brown. After taking them out of the oven, let them cool.
5. Make the fruit filling while the pastry is baking. The mixed berries, honey, lemon juice, and vanilla essence should all be combined in a bowl. Gently toss the berries in the honey mixture to coat them.
6. Prepare the whipped cream in another bowl. Stir in the vanilla essence and whip the heavy cream until firm peaks form.
7. Assemble the napoleons after the pastry rectangles have cooled. The first rectangle of pastry serves as the base. A spoonful of the berry mixture is added, followed by a dollop of whipped cream. Repeat the process with another pastry rectangle, additional berries, and whipped cream
8. Add a final layer of whipped cream on top when all the pastry and filling have been layered.
9. As a finishing touch, sprinkle powdered sugar over the top.
10. Serve your Einkorn Breakfast Fruit Napoleon right away and savor it!

Einkorn Breakfast Fruit Éclair:

Ingredients:

For the eclair shells:

- 1/2 cup water
- Four tablespoons unsalted butter
- 1/2 cup all-purpose einkorn flour
- Two large eggs

For the fruit filling:

- 1 cup whipped cream
- 1 cup mixed fruits (e.g., strawberries, kiwi, and mango), diced
- 2 tablespoons powdered sugar
- One teaspoon of vanilla extract

Instructions:

1. Bring water and butter to a boil in a small saucepan. Add the einkorn flour and whisk well until a smooth ball forms.
2. Take it off the fire and give it some time to cool. Once the dough is smooth, add the eggs gradually, one at a time, beating thoroughly after each addition.
3. Set the oven's temperature to 375°F (190°C).
4. Place the dough inside of a pastry bag with a sizable round tip. Eclair shells 4 inches long should be piped onto parchment paper-lined baking sheets.
5. Bake the eclairs in the hot oven for about 30 minutes or until they are puffy and golden brown. Give them time to cool.
6. Prepare the fruit filling by combining whipped cream, diced mixed fruits, powdered sugar, and vanilla essence while the shells cool.
7. Split the eclair shells in half lengthwise after they have cooled. After adding the fruit and cream mixture to the bottom half, place the top halves back on.
8. You can drizzle on chocolate ganache to go even more indulgent.
9. Dish up your Einkorn Breakfast Fruit Eclair and savor it!

Einkorn Breakfast Fruit Crostini:

Ingredients:

- One baguette, thinly sliced
- Two tablespoons of olive oil
- 1 cup ricotta cheese
- 1 cup mixed berries (e.g., blueberries, raspberries)
- Honey for drizzling
- Fresh mint leaves for garnish

Instructions:

1. Set the oven's temperature to 350°F (175°C).
2. Place the baguette slices on a baking pan and brush them with olive oil. They should be toasted in the oven for 5-7 minutes or until crisp and gently brown.
3. Whip the ricotta cheese to a smooth consistency while the crostini are toasting.
4. After baking the crostini, let them cool somewhat, and then generously fill each slice with ricotta cheese.
5. Add mixed berries to the ricotta and sprinkle honey over the top.
6. Add fresh mint leaves as a garnish.
7. Use your Einkorn Breakfast Fruit Crostini as a tasty breakfast treat or appetizer.

Einkorn Breakfast Fruit Sliders:

Ingredients:

For the sliders:

- 12 small Einkorn breakfast rolls
- Six eggs
- Six slices of cooked bacon

- Six slices of cheddar cheese
- Salt and pepper to taste

For the fruit topping:

- 1 cup mixed fruit (e.g., pineapple, strawberries, kiwi), diced
- Two tablespoons of maple syrup

Instructions:

1. Set the oven's temperature to 350°F (175°C).
2. The Einkorn breakfast buns should be divided in half and arranged on a baking pan.
3. Whip the eggs in a bowl and season with salt and pepper. In a pan, scramble the eggs until they are the proper doneness.
4. Top the bottom half of each bun with a slice of cheddar cheese and a cooked bacon slice.
5. Top the cheese and bacon with the scrambled eggs.
6. Place the second half of the rolls on top.
7. Bake the sliders in the hot oven for 10 minutes or until the cheese is melted and the rolls are warm.
8. Prepare the topping by combining the diced fruit and maple syrup in a basin while the sliders are baking.
9. Take the sliders out of the oven when they have finished baking, and serve them with a tablespoon of the fruit topping.
10. Enjoy your fruit sliders from Einkorn Breakfast!

Einkorn Breakfast Fruit Stuffed Crepes:

Ingredients:

For the crepes:

- 1 cup Einkorn flour
- Two large eggs
- 1 1/2 cups milk
- Two tablespoons melted butter
- 1/4 teaspoon salt

For the fruit filling:

- 2 cups mixed berries (e.g., strawberries, blueberries, raspberries)
- 1/4 cup powdered sugar
- One teaspoon of lemon juice

For serving:

- Whipped cream (optional)
- Maple syrup (optional)

Instructions:

1. Blend Einkorn flour, eggs, milk, melted butter, and salt in a food processor. Blend the batter up to smoothness. Give it 30 minutes to relax.
2. Heat a crepe pan or nonstick skillet over medium heat. Use butter to lightly grease it.
3. Drop a little crepe batter into the skillet and swirl it around to evenly coat the bottom. Cook until the edges lift, which should take 1-2 minutes.

4. Turn the crepe over and cook the second side for 1-2 minutes. Continue by using the remaining batter.
5. Combine the mixed berries, powdered sugar, and lemon juice in a bowl to make the fruit filling.
6. Place the fruit filling in the center of each crepe, fold it into quarters, and serve.
7. You can drizzle some maple syrup and add some whipped cream on top.
8. Enjoy your fruit-stuffed crepes from Einkorn Breakfast!

Einkorn Breakfast Fruit Crepe Cake:

Ingredients:

For the crepes:

- 1 cup Einkorn flour
- Two large eggs
- 1 1/2 cups milk
- Two tablespoons melted butter
- 1/4 teaspoon salt

For the filling:

- 2 cups mixed berries (e.g., strawberries, blueberries, raspberries)
- 1 cup whipped cream
- Two tablespoons powdered sugar
- One teaspoon of vanilla extract

Instructions:

1. Combine the Einkorn flour, eggs, milk, melted butter, and salt in a blender to make the crepe batter. Give the batter 30 minutes to rest.

2. Put a nonstick skillet on the stovetop at medium heat. Use butter to lightly grease it.
3. Drop a little crepe batter into the skillet and swirl it around to evenly coat the bottom. Cook until the edges lift, which should take 1-2 minutes.
4. Turn the crepe over and cook the second side for 1-2 minutes. Continue until all of the batter has been used. Twelve crepes should be about right.
5. Make the filling while the crepes are cooling. Combine the vanilla extract, powdered sugar, and mixed berries.
6. Whip the cream in another dish until stiff peaks form.
7. To put the crepe cake together, put one crepe on a serving plate and cover it with a thin layer of whipped cream. Spread out a dollop of the berry mixture on top. Continue piling crepes, whipped cream, and berries until all the crepes have been utilized.
8. To help the crepe cake solidify, place it in the refrigerator for at least 30 minutes.
9. Distribute and enjoy your Einkorn Breakfast Fruit Crepe Cake!

Einkorn Breakfast Fruit Pancake Stack:

Ingredients:

For the pancakes:

- 1 cup Einkorn flour
- Two tablespoons sugar
- One teaspoon of baking powder
- 1/2 teaspoon baking soda
- 1/4 teaspoon salt
- 1 cup buttermilk
- One large egg

- Two tablespoons melted butter
- One teaspoon of vanilla extract

For the fruit topping:

- 2 cups mixed berries (e.g., blueberries, raspberries, blackberries)
- Two tablespoons honey
- One teaspoon of lemon juice

Instructions:

1. Combine Einkorn flour, sugar, baking soda, baking powder, and salt in a mixing dish.
2. Combine buttermilk, egg, melted butter, and vanilla essence in a separate basin.
3. Mix the dry ingredients briefly after adding the liquid components. Give the batter some time to rest.
4. Lightly oil a griddle or skillet with cooking spray or butter and heat it over medium-high heat.
5. Spoon parts of the batter measuring 1/4 cup onto the grill to make pancakes. Cook until surface bubbles appear, then flip and cook until both sides are golden brown.
6. Mix the mixed berries, honey, and lemon juice in a separate bowl to make the fruit topping.
7. Arrange the pancakes in layers on a serving plate, sandwiching the fruit topping in the middle.
8. If desired, drizzle more honey over the top.
9. Present your fruit pancake stack from the Einkorn Breakfast, and savor it!

Einkorn Breakfast Fruit Dutch Baby:

Ingredients:

- Three large eggs
- 1/2 cup Einkorn flour
- 1/2 cup milk
- Two tablespoons sugar
- 1/4 teaspoon salt
- 1/2 teaspoon vanilla extract
- Two tablespoons unsalted butter
- 1 cup mixed berries (e.g., blueberries, strawberries)
- Powdered sugar for dusting
- Maple syrup for serving

Instructions:

1. Set the oven's temperature to 425°F (220°C).
2. Add eggs, Einkorn flour, milk, sugar, salt, and vanilla extract to a blender. Until smooth, blend.
3. Put the butter in a 10-inch ovenproof skillet and heat the oven to a sizzling temperature.
4. Pour the batter into the hot, melted butter in the skillet. Return the skillet to the oven right away.
5. Bake the Dutch baby for 15 to 20 minutes or until it puffs up and turns golden.
6. Combine the mixed berries in a basin and bake the Dutch baby.
7. Take the Dutch baby out of the oven and sprinkle the mixed berries.
8. Sprinkle with icing sugar, then drizzle with maple syrup.
9. Enjoy your Fruit Dutch Baby Einkorn Breakfast!

Einkorn Breakfast Fruit Blintzes:

Ingredients:

For the blintzes:

- 1 cup Einkorn flour
- Two large eggs
- 1 cup milk
- Two tablespoons melted butter
- 1/4 teaspoon salt

For the filling:

- 1 cup ricotta cheese
- 1 cup mixed berries (e.g., raspberries, blueberries)
- Two tablespoons powdered sugar
- One teaspoon of lemon zest

For topping:

- Mixed berries
- Powdered sugar

Instructions:

1. Blend Einkorn flour, eggs, milk, melted butter, and salt in a food processor. Until smooth, blend. Give the batter 20 to 30 minutes to rest.
2. Put a nonstick skillet on the stovetop at medium heat. Use butter to lightly grease it.
3. Pour a tiny amount of batter onto the skillet to produce thin crepes. Turn the pan over and cook for 1-2 minutes after swirling the batter to evenly coat the bottom. Continue until all of the batter has been used.

4. To make the filling, combine ricotta cheese, mixed berries, powdered sugar, and lemon zest in a bowl.
5. Spoon a small filling onto each crepe before rolling it up.
6. Add more mixed berries and a sprinkle of powdered sugar on top of your Einkorn Breakfast Fruit Blintzes before serving.

Einkorn Breakfast Fruit Waffles:

Ingredients:
- 2 cups Einkorn flour
- Two tablespoons sugar
- One tablespoon of baking powder
- 1/2 teaspoon salt
- Two large eggs
- 1 3/4 cups milk
- 1/2 cup melted butter
- One teaspoon of vanilla extract
- 1 cup mixed berries (e.g., strawberries, blueberries)

Instructions:
1. Set your waffle maker to the recommended temperature by the manufacturer.
2. Combine Einkorn flour, sugar, baking soda, and salt in a bowl.
3. Beat the eggs in a separate basin, then stir in the milk, melted butter, and vanilla essence. Mix thoroughly.
4. Mix the dry ingredients briefly after adding the liquid components. The berries are mingled in now.
5. Spoon the batter onto the waffle iron that has been prepared, and cook the waffles until they are crisp and golden brown.

6. Add more mixed berries and maple syrup to your Einkorn Breakfast Fruit Waffles before serving them.

Einkorn Breakfast Fruit French Toast:

Ingredients:

- Eight slices of Einkorn bread
- Four large eggs
- 1 cup milk
- Two tablespoons sugar
- 1/2 teaspoon vanilla extract
- 1/4 teaspoon ground cinnamon
- Mixed berries (e.g., strawberries, blueberries) for topping
- Maple syrup for serving

Instructions:

1. In a small bowl, combine eggs, milk, sugar, vanilla essence, and ground cinnamon.
2. Lightly grease a griddle or large skillet with cooking spray or butter and heat it over medium-high heat.
3. Coat both sides of each piece of Einkorn bread by dipping it into the egg mixture.
4. Place the moistened bread on the hot grill and cook for two to three minutes per side or until golden brown.
5. Drizzle maple syrup over your Einkorn Breakfast Fruit French Toast and top with a heaping serving of mixed berries.

Einkorn Breakfast Fruit Bread Pudding:

Ingredients:

- 4 cups cubed Einkorn bread
- 1 cup mixed berries (e.g., raspberries, blackberries)

- Four large eggs
- 1 1/2 cups milk
- 1/2 cup heavy cream
- 1/2 cup sugar
- One teaspoon of vanilla extract
- 1/4 teaspoon ground cinnamon
- Powdered sugar for dusting

Instructions:

1. Set the oven's temperature to 350°F (175°C). Butter a baking pan.
2. Combine the cubed Einkorn bread and mixed berries in a big basin. Put this mixture in the baking pan that has been buttered.
3. In a separate basin, combine eggs, milk, heavy cream, sugar, vanilla essence, and ground cinnamon

4. Pour the egg mixture into the baking dish with the bread and berries. To ensure that all of the bread is submerged in the mixture, gently press down.
5. Allow the bread pudding to rest for 10 to 15 minutes so that the bread can soak up the liquid.
6. Bake in the preheated oven for 35 to 40 minutes or until the pudding is set and the top is golden brown.
7. Take it out of the oven, let it cool, and then dust it with powdered sugar.

Einkorn Breakfast Fruit Strudel:

Ingredients:

For the strudel:

- One sheet of puff pastry

- 1 cup mixed berries (e.g., strawberries, blueberries, raspberries)
- Two tablespoons sugar
- One tablespoon cornstarch
- 1/2 teaspoon vanilla extract
- One egg (for egg wash)
- Powdered sugar for dusting

Instructions:

1. Set the oven's temperature to 375°F (190°C).
2. Combine mixed berries, cornstarch, sugar, and vanilla extract in a bowl. Toss the berries carefully to coat them.
3. Roll out the puff pastry sheet into a rectangle on a lightly dusted surface.
4. Position the berry mixture in the pastry's center.
5. To enclose the berry mixture, fold the sides of the crust over and fork-seal the borders.
6. Beat the egg and drizzle it over the strudel's top.
7. Bake the strudel in the preheated oven for 25 to 30 minutes or until the filling is bubbling and the strudel is golden brown.
8. Just before serving, sprinkle with powdered sugar.

Einkorn Breakfast Fruit Danish Braid:

Ingredients:

For the Danish braid:

- One sheet of puff pastry
- 1 cup mixed berries (e.g., strawberries, blueberries, raspberries)
- 1/4 cup cream cheese, softened

- Two tablespoons powdered sugar
- One egg (for egg wash)

For the glaze:

- 1/2 cup powdered sugar
- 1-2 tablespoons milk
- 1/2 teaspoon vanilla extract

Instructions:

1. Set the oven's temperature to 375°F (190°C).
2. Roll out the puff pastry sheet into a rectangle on a lightly dusted surface.
3. Combine cream cheese and powdered sugar in a bowl and stir until combined. Over the puff pastry's center, spread this mixture.
4. Top the cream cheese mixture with the mixed berries.
5. Trim a border around the filling before cutting diagonal strips from the puff pastry's sides.
6. Fold the pastry's top and bottom edges over the filling, and then begin braiding the pastry strips over the filling on an angle, alternating the sides.
7. Whisk the egg and spread it over the braid's top.
8. Bake in the oven for 20 to 25 minutes or until the braid is golden brown.
9. Make the glaze by combining powdered sugar, milk, and vanilla essence and whisking until smooth while the braid bakes.
10. After baking the braid, please remove it from the oven and cover it with glaze.
11. Cut your Einkorn Breakfast Fruit Danish Braid into slices and serve it!

Einkorn Breakfast Fruit Kolache:

Ingredients:

For the kolache dough:

- 2 1/4 teaspoons active dry yeast
- 1/4 cup warm water
- 1/4 cup sugar
- 1/2 cup milk, lukewarm
- 1/4 cup unsalted butter, melted
- Two large eggs
- 3 1/2 cups Einkorn flour
- 1/2 teaspoon salt

For the fruit filling:

- 1 cup mixed fruit preserves (e.g., apricot, cherry, or strawberry)

Instructions:

1. Combine the yeast, sugar, and warm water in a small basin. Till it starts to foam, let it a few minutes to sit.
2. Combine the yeast mixture, lukewarm milk, melted butter, and eggs in a sizable mixing basin.
3. Add salt and Einkorn flour to the mixture and stir until a dough forms.
4. To make the dough smooth and elastic, knead it for about 5 minutes on a floured board.
5. After putting the dough in a greased basin and covering it with a kitchen towel, allow it to rise for one to two hours or until it has doubled.
6. Set the oven's temperature to 350°F (175°C).
7. Divide the dough into equal halves after punching it down.

8. Form each part into a ball, then set each ball on a parchment-lined baking sheet.
9. Press your thumb into the center of each dough ball to create an indentation, then place a spoonful of mixed fruit preserves within.
10. Bake the kolaches in the oven for 15 to 18 minutes or until golden brown.
11. Before serving your Einkorn Breakfast Fruit Kolache, let them cool slightly.

Einkorn Breakfast Fruit Babka:
Ingredients:

For the babka dough:

- 4 cups Einkorn flour
- 1/2 cup sugar
- 2 1/4 teaspoons active dry yeast
- 1 cup warm milk
- Two large eggs
- 1/2 cup unsalted butter, softened
- 1/2 teaspoon salt

For the fruit filling:

- 1 cup mixed dried fruit (e.g., raisins, currants, apricots)
- 1/4 cup sugar
- Two tablespoons melted butter
- One teaspoon ground cinnamon

Instructions:
1. Combine the yeast, sugar, and warm milk in a small basin. Till it starts to foam, let it a few minutes to sit.

2. Combine salt and Einkorn flour in a sizable mixing dish.
3. Combine the flour mixture with the yeast, eggs, and softened butter. Mix until a dough forms.
4. To make the dough smooth and elastic, knead it for about 5 minutes on a floured board.
5. After putting the dough in a greased basin and covering it with a kitchen towel, allow it to rise for one to two hours or until it has doubled.
6. Set the oven's temperature to 350°F (175°C).
7. Mix the mixed dried fruit, sugar, melted butter, and ground cinnamon in a bowl to make the filling.
8. Create a large rectangle out of the dough.
9. Evenly distribute the fruit filling over the dough.
10. To form a log, tightly roll the dough, starting from the long side.
11. Split the log lengthwise to reveal the fruit contents.
12. Twist the two pieces of dough together, then put them into a loaf pan that has been buttered.
13. Bake for 35 to 40 minutes in a preheated oven or until the babka is golden brown and hollow to the touch.
14. Before slicing and serving your Einkorn Breakfast Fruit Babka, allow it to cool.

Einkorn Breakfast Fruit Beignets:
Ingredients:

For the beignets:

- 1 cup Einkorn flour
- One tablespoon sugar
- 1/2 teaspoon baking powder
- 1/4 teaspoon salt
- 1/2 cup milk

- One large egg
- 1/2 cup mixed berries (e.g., blueberries, raspberries)
- Vegetable oil for frying
- Powdered sugar for dusting

Instructions:

1. Combine Einkorn flour, sugar, baking soda, and salt in a mixing dish.
2. In another bowl, thoroughly mix the milk and egg.
3. Mix the batter until smooth after adding the wet components to the dry ones.
4. Gently incorporate the berries.
5. Bring a big, heavy saucepan with about 2 inches of vegetable oil to 350°F (175°C).
6. Spoonfuls of the batter should be dropped into the hot oil and fried until golden brown, flipping as necessary.
7. Using a slotted spoon, remove the beignets from the oil and place them on paper towels to drain.
8. Before serving your Einkorn Breakfast Fruit Beignets, sprinkle with powdered sugar!

Einkorn Breakfast Fruit Puff Pastry:

Ingredients:

- One sheet of puff pastry
- 1 cup mixed berries (e.g., strawberries, blueberries, raspberries)
- Two tablespoons sugar
- One tablespoon cornstarch
- 1/2 teaspoon vanilla extract
- One egg (for egg wash)
- Powdered sugar for dusting

Instructions:

1. Set the oven's temperature to 375°F (190°C).
2. Roll out the puff pastry sheet into a rectangle on a lightly dusted surface.
3. Combine the mixed berries, cornstarch, sugar, and vanilla essence in a bowl.
4. Center the puff pastry with the berry mixture.
5. To enclose the berry mixture, fold the sides of the crust over and fork-seal the borders.
6. Whisk the egg and spread it over the puff pastry's top.
7. Bake the pastry in the oven for 20 to 25 minutes or until golden brown.
8. Before serving, sprinkle your Einkorn Breakfast Fruit Puff Pastry with powdered sugar!

Einkorn Breakfast Fruit Croissant Ring:

Ingredients:

- Two sheets of puff pastry
- 1 cup mixed berries (e.g., blueberries, raspberries)
- Two tablespoons sugar
- One tablespoon cornstarch
- 1/2 teaspoon vanilla extract
- One egg (for egg wash)
- Powdered sugar for dusting

Instructions:

1. Line a baking sheet with parchment paper and preheat your oven to 425°F (220°C).
2. Combine Einkorn flour, sugar, baking soda, and salt in a bowl.
3. Combine the dry ingredients with the cooled, diced butter. Work the butter into the flour mixture with a

pastry cutter or your fingers until it resembles coarse crumbs.
4. Gently incorporate the berries.
5. Combine the heavy cream, egg, and vanilla extract in another basin.
6. Mix the dry ingredients briefly after adding the liquid components.
7. Spread the dough out onto a floured surface and give it a couple of gentle kneads to bring it together.
8. Form a circle out of the dough that is approximately an inch thick.
9. Cut the dough into eight wedges and arrange them on the baking sheet that has been prepared.
10. Bake the scones in the oven for 12 to 15 minutes or until golden brown.
11. Before serving your Einkorn Breakfast Fruit Scones, let the scones cool somewhat.

Einkorn Breakfast Fruit Danish Twists:

Ingredients:
- One sheet of puff pastry
- 1/2 cup mixed berries (e.g., strawberries, blueberries)
- Two tablespoons sugar
- One egg (for egg wash)
- Powdered sugar for dusting

Instructions:
1. Set the oven's temperature to 375°F (190°C).
2. Roll out the puff pastry sheet into a rectangle on a lightly dusted surface.
3. Thoroughly blend sugar and mixed berries in a bowl.
4. Divide the pastry sheet into squares or smaller rectangles.

5. Fill each rectangle or square with a spoonful of the berry mixture, allowing some room around the edges.
6. Fold the remaining pastry over the berries to form a triangle or half-moon.
7. Seal the pastries by pressing the edges.
8. After beating the egg, brush it on top of the pastries.
9. Bake the pastries in the oven for 15 to 20 minutes or until golden brown.
10. Before serving your Einkorn Breakfast Fruit Danish Twists, sprinkle with powdered sugar!

Einkorn Breakfast Fruit Pinwheels:

Ingredients:
- One sheet of puff pastry
- 1 cup mixed berries (e.g., blueberries, raspberries)
- Two tablespoons sugar
- One egg (for egg wash)
- Powdered sugar for dusting

Instructions:
1. Set the oven's temperature to 375°F (190°C).
2. Roll out the puff pastry sheet into a rectangle on a lightly dusted surface.
3. Thoroughly blend sugar and mixed berries in a bowl.
4. Evenly cover the puff pastry with the berry mixture.
5. To form a log, roll the puff pastry starting at one end.
6. Cut the log into pinwheels of the same size.
7. Arrange the pinwheels on a parchment-lined baking sheet.
8. After whisking the egg, brush the pinwheels' tops with it.
9. Bake the pinwheels in the oven for 15 to 20 minutes or until golden brown.

10. Before serving your Einkorn Breakfast Fruit Pinwheels, sprinkle with powdered sugar!

Einkorn Breakfast Fruit Scones:

Ingredients:

- 2 cups Einkorn flour
- 1/4 cup sugar
- One tablespoon of baking powder
- 1/2 teaspoon salt
- 1/2 cup unsalted butter, cold and cubed
- 2/3 cup mixed berries (e.g., blueberries, raspberries)
- 2/3 cup heavy cream
- One large egg
- One teaspoon of vanilla extract

Instructions:

1. Line a baking sheet with parchment paper and preheat your oven to 425°F (220°C).
2. Combine Einkorn flour, sugar, baking soda, and salt in a bowl.
3. Combine the dry ingredients with the cooled, diced butter. Work the butter into the flour mixture with a pastry cutter or your fingers until it resembles coarse crumbs.
4. Gently incorporate the berries.
5. Combine the heavy cream, egg, and vanilla extract in another basin.
6. Mix the dry ingredients briefly after adding the liquid components.
7. Spread the dough out onto a floured surface and give it a couple of gentle kneads to bring it together.
8. Form a circle out of the dough that is approximately an inch thick.

9. Cut the dough into eight wedges and arrange them on the baking sheet that has been prepared.
10. Bake the scones in the oven for 12 to 15 minutes or until golden brown.
11. Before serving your Einkorn Breakfast Fruit Scones, let the scones cool somewhat.

Einkorn Breakfast Fruit Biscuits:

Ingredients:

- 2 cups Einkorn flour
- 1/4 cup sugar
- Two teaspoons of baking powder
- 1/2 teaspoon salt
- 1/2 cup unsalted butter, cold and cubed
- 2/3 cup mixed berries (e.g., blueberries, raspberries)
- 2/3 cup milk
- One teaspoon of vanilla extract

Instructions:

1. Line a baking sheet with parchment paper and preheat your oven to 425°F (220°C).
2. Combine Einkorn flour, sugar, baking soda, and salt in a bowl.
3. Combine the dry ingredients with the cooled, diced butter. Work the butter into the flour mixture with a pastry cutter or your fingers until it resembles coarse crumbs.
4. Gently incorporate the berries.
5. Combine the milk and vanilla essence in a separate basin.
6. Mix the dry ingredients briefly after adding the liquid components.

7. Spread the dough out onto a floured surface and give it a couple of gentle kneads to bring it together.
8. Form a circle out of the dough that is approximately an inch thick.
9. Cut biscuit shapes from the dough using a biscuit cutter and arrange them on the lined baking sheet.
10. Bake the biscuits in the oven for 12 to 15 minutes or until golden brown.
11. Before serving your Einkorn Breakfast Fruit Biscuits, let the biscuits cool somewhat.

Einkorn Breakfast Fruit Tea Bread:

Ingredients:

- 2 cups Einkorn flour
- 1/2 cup sugar
- Two teaspoons of baking powder
- 1/2 teaspoon salt
- 1/2 cup unsalted butter, softened
- 2/3 cup mixed berries (e.g., blueberries, raspberries)
- 2/3 cup milk
- Two large eggs
- One teaspoon of vanilla extract

Instructions:

1. Grease a loaf pan that measures 9x5 inches and preheat your oven to 350°F (175°C).
2. Combine Einkorn flour, sugar, baking soda, and salt in a bowl.
3. Beat the softened butter until it is creamy in a separate bowl.
4. Beat the butter with the eggs and vanilla essence until thoroughly mixed.

5. Stirring until just incorporated, add the dry ingredients in small amounts, alternating with the milk.
6. Gently incorporate the berries.
7. Fill the prepared loaf pan with the batter.
8. Bake for 45 to 55 minutes in a preheated oven or until a toothpick inserted in the center comes out clean.
9. After the tea bread has cooled in the pan for ten minutes, move it to a wire rack to finish cooling.
10. Cut your Einkorn Breakfast Fruit Tea Bread into slices and serve it!

Einkorn Breakfast Fruit Coffee Cake:

Ingredients:

For the cake:

- 2 cups Einkorn flour
- 1 cup sugar
- One teaspoon of baking powder
- 1/2 teaspoon baking soda
- 1/2 teaspoon salt
- 1/2 cup unsalted butter, softened
- Two large eggs
- 1 cup sour cream
- One teaspoon of vanilla extract

For the fruit topping:

- 2 cups mixed berries (e.g., strawberries, blueberries, raspberries)
- 1/4 cup sugar
- One tablespoon cornstarch

For the streusel topping:

- 1/2 cup Einkorn flour
- 1/2 cup brown sugar
- 1/4 cup unsalted butter, melted
- 1/2 teaspoon ground cinnamon

Instructions:

1. Grease a 9x13-inch baking pan and preheat your oven to 350°F (175°C).
2. Combine the mixed berries, sugar, and cornstarch in a bowl to make the fruit topping. Place aside.
3. To make the streusel topping, combine the Einkorn flour, brown sugar, melted butter, and ground cinnamon in a separate basin. Mix until the mixture resembles crumbly food. Place aside.
4. Combine Einkorn flour, sugar, baking soda, baking powder, and salt in a sizable mixing basin.
5. Beat the softened butter until smooth in a separate dish. Mix well after adding the eggs, sour cream, and vanilla extract.
6. Blend the dry ingredients until smooth after incorporating the wet components gradually.
7. Spoon the cake batter equally into the prepared baking pan.
8. Top the cake batter with the fruit topping.
9. Cover the fruit equally with the streusel topping.
10. Bake for 45 to 50 minutes in a preheated oven or until a toothpick inserted in the center comes out clean.
11. Let the coffee cake cool completely before serving it with fruit for Einkorn Breakfast!

Made in United States
Troutdale, OR
01/22/2024

17058483R00156